ADVANCE PRAISE

"Chad Willardson is much more than a financial ninja; his entire career is dedicated to helping entrepreneurs elevate their life and their business! In *Wealth Wired Differently*, Chad unveils the accelerators for entrepreneurial success when you partner with financial experts who are wired just like you."

—**Randy Garn,** *NYT* bestselling Author & Investor

"Chad isn't just a financial advisor to me, he's a role model and mentor, who challenges me to think and act BIGGER. He inspires and coaches me on how to live an abundant 10x life as an entrepreneur."

—**Dr. Benjamin Hardy,** Organizational Psychologist, Co-Author of *10X is Easier Than 2X*

"Entrepreneurial families are so unique; they see the world so differently, especially in regards to money and success. In *Wealth Wired Differently*, Chad shows us how entrepreneurial families really prosper when working with financial experts who live in that same entrepreneurial world that they do, where possibilities are endless!"

—**Shannon Waller,** Director & Coach at Strategic Coach®

"The disconnect between entrepreneurs and financial advisors has always been an obstacle that seemed unsolvable. As entrepreneurs, we don't want the same traditional financial advice that everyone else gets. There are very few wealth advisory professionals like Chad who understand us because he's one of us. *Wealth Wired Differently* clearly outlines why this matters to entrepreneurs like you and me."

—**Chad Johnson,** Entrepreneur & Business Coach

WEALTH
WIRED
DIFFERENTLY

WEALTH WIRED DIFFERENTLY

7 Advantages Entrepreneurs Miss Out on When Taking Financial Advice from Non-Entrepreneurs

CHAD WILLARDSON, CRPC®, AWMA®

WEALTH WIRED DIFFERENTLY

7 Advantages Entrepreneurs Miss Out on When Taking Financial Advice from Non-Entrepreneurs

Interior Layout and Design by Stephanie Anderson
Book Cover Design by Abigael Elliott

ISBN:
979-8-89165-098-5 *Paperback*
979-8-89165-099-2 *Hardback*
979-8-89165-100-5 *E-book*

Published by:
Streamline Books
Kansas City, MO
streamlinebookspublishing.com

STREAMLINE
B O O K S

To my wife, Amber; my kids, McKinley, Pierce, Sterling, Bentley, and Beckham; and my parents and close friends, who essentially are along for the roller coaster ride of my entrepreneurship and big new ideas. You've seen and heard the excitement of new opportunities and ideas, followed by the stresses, the grind, the ups and downs, the disappointments—and also the massive wins. You've celebrated the successes and have shown confidence despite uncertainty every time I decided it was time for a big new jump!

I also dedicate this book to each of you out there who were told your ideas were crazy and wouldn't work, who embrace the uncertainty, who take the chances that others are scared to take, who see opportunity and abundance in everything, who refuse to take no for an answer, who are willing to sacrifice security and certainty in exchange for the chance of success and impact in the world.

This is for you.

CONTENTS

FOREWORD

By Chad Johnson, Entrepreneur and Business Coach

I have been an entrepreneur for 46 years, starting at 7 years old when I took the avocados from the trees in our backyard in Southern California and started selling them door to door to our neighbors. The entrepreneurial journey is a lifelong adventure to me. I love this approach to building a life and a career because as entrepreneurs, the world is our oyster. We see opportunity and possibility everywhere. When we face a challenge or a question, we are open to and seek out multiple solutions, not just a single one.

We get excited by investment opportunities that might be a little "outside the box." But that makes sense because in-the-box thinking definitely didn't get us here in the first place. Our risk threshold is different. Playing in new spaces is exciting. We're just wired differently—which is why this book title makes so much sense.

Traditional financial advice just isn't designed for that, and it's frustrating. It's designed to take your cash out of anywhere else you have it and put it into buckets the traditional advisor understands and can sell you. This isn't "bad," necessarily. If you're a W-2 employee or a highly paid doctor or lawyer, for example, traditional advice about retirement planning and leveraging the market might make sense. There's nothing wrong with that. It just felt limiting to me.

As an entrepreneur myself, I want financial advice that speaks to me as a whole person: support from a professional standpoint when I have questions about my business strategy, support from a personal standpoint when I have questions about navigating my family life as an entrepreneur, support from a financial standpoint when I have questions about making my next big move.

I want to have a high-level conversation about those things with my financial team. I want them to bounce back with advice they can offer from personal experience to help me grow during up times and help me figure out my next best move during not-so-up times.

It's more than a want, actually. It's a *need* if we want to reach true holistic wealth and freedom. I knew I wasn't satisfied with the advice I'd gotten before, but I didn't know this entrepreneur-to-entrepreneur approach was even a possibility until I met Chad and heard his passion for helping entrepreneurs do wealth management differently. That's when the walls came down and I finally felt supported and understood. It was like there had been a language barrier all along, and finally someone "got it."

In this book, Chad walks you through seven advantages you can experience by working with an entrepreneurial advisor. Unselfishly, he knows it doesn't even have to be him (though it could be). He's giving this information away so you can learn some strategies and walk away inspired and empowered to find your best-fitting financial team. One who gets you completely!

This book, in short, is music to an entrepreneur's ears.

INTRODUCTION

Being an entrepreneur means looking at things differently. It means *doing* things differently—big things, usually.

For some reason, it also means you probably heard things like, "When are you going to get a *real job*?" when you were just starting out.

I can't tell you how many times that's been said to me or about me and people close to me. At a certain point, you have to learn to tune out the people asking, "When are you going to get serious about your career?" or saying, "There's no way that idea's gonna work." No matter how many times you've heard it, though, there's still a sting to being misunderstood. That's why, in a way, we're the misfits of the world. Because we do things our own way. We look around at problems and frustrations and see possibilities and new opportunities. Accepting the status quo isn't in our DNA.

This major difference is the reason you've probably always felt like the odd one out. Most traditional advice doesn't sit well with you, and you've never considered yourself to be someone who just goes along with what "everybody else is doing." I'm sure you've had that feeling like I have, when everyone around you thought a certain way or was willing to accept an outcome that wasn't ideal, but something inside you was restless because you knew there had to be a better way.

As an entrepreneur, you've chosen to step out of the crowd and create your own path. One area entrepreneurs express a lot of frustration around is working with "financial advisors." But think about this: most financial advisors are not true entrepreneurs themselves. For our purposes, we'll call these traditional advisors "employee advisors" throughout this book because that's what they are: they're financial advisors who are employed by someone else—typically a big bank, brokerage firm, or large insurance agency. We'll call advisors who are entrepreneurs "entrepreneurial advisors," meaning they, like you and I, own one or more businesses that they started themselves. Think about the big picture for a second: How could a traditional employee advisor really understand you and how you think? How can they guide you down this unique entrepreneurial journey if it's a path they've never been on? As entrepreneurs, who should you be taking advice from? As a father of five kids, I've always said that you don't really know what it's like to be a parent until you have your own kids. It's hard to describe the feeling. You can read books about and watch videos about parenthood, but until you actually hold your own child in your arms, you just don't understand it. Feels a lot like entrepreneurship. You can talk about it, read about it, and even listen to podcasts about it . . . but until you burn the boats of being an employee and suddenly carry the entire burden on your own shoulders, you don't understand it.

Introduction

Employee advisors offering traditional financial advice will talk all day about *the markets, the markets, the markets.* Maybe you've sat through meetings where an overdressed business professional in their corporate uniform was talking about the stock market, asset allocation, diversification, and the headline economic news with their slide deck full of pie charts and graphs, and you were wondering, *What am I doing here? What are they talking about?* Maybe your mind was drifting off into that new business idea or collaboration . . . or even some new business challenge you needed to tackle as soon as this boring meeting was over. My point is that there's a major language barrier between employee advisors and entrepreneurs, and that's a problem.

To the entrepreneur's ear, employee advisors sound like the teacher to Charlie Brown in the classic cartoon *Peanuts*: "Wah wa wa wah wa wa." If you're taking advice from a traditional employee advisor who hasn't ever started, grown, led, and/or sold a business, you're listening to someone who doesn't know where you've been and can't fully comprehend where you want to go.

Thankfully, there's an alternative. With an entrepreneurial advisor, there's no language barrier. If you work with someone who is fluent in entrepreneurship, you'll be understood, and you'll likely go farther and faster financially and in terms of lifestyle freedom.

EXPERIENCE MATTERS

I have twenty-three years in the wealth management industry. I'm an author for *Entrepreneur* magazine and on the Forbes Business Council. I own many different companies that I've started or invested in, and I've written four other books about investing for high-net-worth entrepreneurs and families. I've been an outside-the-box thinker since I was little.

Having started as an employee of Merrill Lynch—where I had a regular W-2 paycheck, benefits, and generous employee stock options—I escaped from the corporate world and Wall Street to become an entrepreneur in 2011. Because of that experience, I know how to speak the traditional "financial advisor" language. As an entrepreneur, I also know a newer, more relevant language that aligns with what people like you and me speak every day. This means I've been on both sides, and I really found my voice once I stepped out of the corporate world (where I didn't fit in, anyway).

As entrepreneurs, we're wired differently, plain and simple. In trying to steward the wealth and value you've generated from your business, you may have had a feeling that something's off with traditional financial advice from your traditional employee advisor. Maybe there's a disconnect that you couldn't quite put your finger on. Instead of encouraging you to get with a rigid, traditional financial program that doesn't actually fit what excites you, in this book, I'm going to share seven *advantages* to the way you approach the world as an entrepreneur and explain the type of financial advice and support that could better serve you.

COLOR OUTSIDE THE LINES

Let's be clear: entrepreneurs don't color within the lines. We never have. In fact, the lines feel restrictive, including the lines within the financial advice industry. That means most likely, if you're an entrepreneur reading this book, you've got a little bit of rule-breaker in you. You've got a little bit of rebel in you. You've got a little bit of "don't tell me what to do." You may be unemployable, and you wear that as a badge of honor.

I get it because I'm absolutely unemployable. The moment you start telling me what I "have" to do, I won't do it. I'll just resist. I can't even explain it, but I think you understand what I'm saying. The traditional financial advice world doesn't work for people like you and me because it tries to be linear and strictly prescriptive with a group of people who have a hard time being told what they can and can't do. When an employee advisor tells an entrepreneur, "You can't do this, you can't invest in this idea, you can't put more money in your business, *can't, can't, can't* . . ." All they're doing is driving a wedge into the relationship. It's misaligned. And a misaligned team doesn't win together very often.

An employee advisor will tell you what you can and can't do if you want to make it to whatever your designated monetary mountain-top is. They try to get everyone to fit inside a box. Their approach relies on lots of rules of thumb, none of which are applicable or acceptable to an exponential-thinking entrepreneur. You don't play by these rules.

You might have been trying to do what you "should" do by following the advice of your employee advisor, but I'll bet something just feels off. You might feel bothered, constrained, or restricted. I've even heard people talk about how they feel hostile toward their financial advisor, but they don't know where else to go. They simply use the same guy or gal that their friend (a non-entrepreneur) recommended to them.

Maybe you haven't pinpointed the problem yet, but you just feel like something isn't working with your current advisor. This book should shed some light on what that problem is and how to fix it.

WHAT YOU'RE MISSING

What do you miss out on by taking wealth and financial advice from non-entrepreneurs? If you settle for the traditional track, where I believe you don't belong, what do you fail to receive?

More than anything, you lose out on the momentum and exponential growth you could achieve if you worked with someone who understood you and shared your vision. As much as you know you need help, when you don't feel understood or in alignment with your financial team, that friction will constantly slow you down.

The difference between you—an entrepreneur—and the average financial advisory client is the difference between exponential thinking and traditional, incremental thinking. You dream big and you take big leaps, against all odds. You're not in the game to make a little bit each month until you retire and claim Social Security. You understand the value of swinging for the fences. You know that not every try will be a home run . . . but you *also know* the ones that are can change your life in ways a regular 9-to-5 paycheck never could.

Employee advisors simply talk about investment accounts, the markets, and what the so-called experts are predicting for the upcoming quarter or year. That's what they do. They print out a thick slide deck of pie charts and graphs about what's happening in your brokerage accounts, then they talk about the latest changes in interest rates and the markets. Meanwhile, our type of entrepreneurial client is dealing with a major business opportunity, a big crisis, or a significant financial or strategic decision within the business . . . and that's all they're thinking about. If you're an entrepreneur working with a financial robot who is just spewing out short-term market statistics, market updates, market statistics, market updates, you're not going to feel supported or heard.

People in the financial services industry tend to get so caught up in caring about all the little upticks and downticks of the markets, but you're dealing with your businesses every day. You're not fixated on what's happening in the stock market. You're thinking about making the next big hire, buying a building, undertaking an expansion, or brainstorming where your next big client will come from. Maybe you have to do some layoffs, and you're worried about how your personal relationships will be affected. That's what you're thinking about. If your advisor doesn't know how to get on your level and talk about those issues, they're not connecting where and when it matters most to you. And ultimately, *you're* the one missing out.

It's not that traditional employee advisors would have different advice for you about your business ideas; they likely wouldn't have *any* advice, because they wouldn't even know how to dig in and ask. They haven't experienced the stress of making payroll when the economy is in the tank and their business is down. There's something much different when you give advice from your own personal experience. Your money strategy and your business strategy are completely connected. Advisors without an entrepreneurial background can't help you see around corners if they don't even know what those corners are.

As a pure entrepreneurial advisor, I think of my role more like a travel guide rather than a travel agent. A travel agent is very transactional. They help you book trips and journeys to places they may never have been. They're trying to sell you a destination they've never even seen! By contrast, a travel *guide* has been up and down the path many times and actually accompanies you on the entire journey, showing you where to go, giving warnings about dangers ahead, advising you what to avoid, and pointing out the beautiful sights you don't want to miss. A travel agent just wants to get you booked and bank their commission, leaving you to go and explore for yourself, because they've never been there and may not be an explorer themselves anyway. An entrepreneur giving entrepreneurs financial advice is more like a travel guide. We're giving you advice based on where we've been before (and what we've learned along the way).

Now, let's talk about how to transform your financial management from the constraining and traditional old way (that fits perfectly for 99 percent of people out there) into the exponential, entrepreneurial style you deserve.

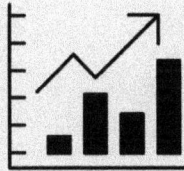

*"Never take your eyes
off the cash flow
because it's the
lifeblood of business."*

—RICHARD BRANSON

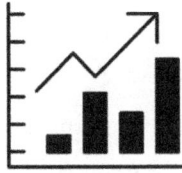

CHAPTER 1

Manage Your Cash Flow Uncertainty with Confidence

Can you be strategic financially when almost nothing—especially future cash flow—is certain or predictable?

That's the life of an entrepreneur.

And the answer, by the way, is yes. You can definitely still be strategic, as long as you're surrounded by professionals who know how to guide you through that uncertainty.

Here's a good example of what this can look like: a new business owner client came to our firm having been referred by their friend. As we dug into their case to see what needed the most attention first, we found out they had large unexpected tax liabilities. This was, obviously, a big concern for them. They weren't prepared for it. They didn't have significant cash in the business account to cover this bill, and it was near the end of the year (with a due date fast approaching).

Roadblock, right? Not with the right creative thinking.

We were able to brainstorm and find a unique idea about how to borrow money to pay for that temporary big expense around the corner. We found a way to leverage one of their seemingly inaccessible investment accounts so that they could receive a line of credit to borrow from, allowing them to pay the multimillion dollar tax bill that came from a planning mistake their previous tax professionals had not accounted for.

Then, as revenues came in during the next 12 months, we helped them work a plan and completely pay off that debt. It was a timely, creative, strategic solution at the just the right time, one that I doubt they would have otherwise found. Without some creative entrepreneurial thinking and advice, they would have been hard-pressed to pay for this temporary, unexpected cash crunch without disrupting the business plans for the following year. Without working with the bank to facilitate the short-term debt solution, they would've been in a very rough financial position and would've had to let go of key personnel on the team.

"I always did something I was a little not ready to do. I think that's how you grow. When there's that moment of 'Wow, I'm not really sure I can do this,' and you push through those moments, that's when you have a breakthrough."

—MARISSA MAYER

Often during the first phase of bringing on an entrepreneur as a new client to our firm, we need to clean up a lot of their financial life because the various aspects of their finances have been viewed in separate silos. Their business financials often haven't been integrated and coordinated with their personal financials. Their business goals and their family goals aren't connected to wealth management decisions or strategies; they've been operating separately. We bring everything together for them, and it's a whole new experience they're not used to. As entrepreneurial advisors, we can talk about both sides (personal finance and business finance) comprehensively, and clients are often not used to that.

PLANNING FOR CASH FLOW

People often ask, "How much should I reinvest into the business? Should I be paying myself more?" How much entrepreneurs should pay themselves is an interesting question. How do you compensate yourself through all the economic and business ups and downs? How much should be left inside your business at the end of the year? How much should you be investing for growth? How much is available for you, the owner, to compensate yourself and invest outside the business versus invest inside the business? Can your cash flow support expanding and hiring?

To figure out the answers to these questions and more, you need a solid cash-flow analysis for your business. You need to understand business financial statements. These are important considerations, and an employee advisor—who earns a regular W-2 paycheck and only really has personal experience and advice for people who receive regular paychecks—may not have a great way to approach them.

The traditional financial advice would be to keep your head down, set aside a fixed amount of money into traditional retirement vehicles, and look at the balance sheet in a very black-and-white, linear way.

Entrepreneurs need to look at cash flow, debt, investing, and risk differently from W-2 employees. Most entrepreneurs start the year having absolutely no idea how much they're going to personally earn in the next twelve months. Additionally, they may not even know exactly how much they earned last year (until their books are done and they can see how it all shook out). That's because it's not an easy, straightforward number to look at on a paystub. That's not how running your own business works. There are so many other factors inside the business finances that are hard to have a clear perspective on without expert help.

Employee advisors know how to work with paystub people, who represent about 133 million people in the US alone. Their strategies are much simpler, like balancing a checkbook. Those work fine if you have a single document that can show you exactly what you earned for the year (and if you can guess with a high level of confidence what you will earn the following year).

Traditional financial advice would say if you're going to make $100,000 and will have $80,000 of expenses and taxes for the year, you should aim to save and invest $20,000 per year. Those are example figures, but the point is to show you how it's a very simple formula being used to calculate and project forward.

Entrepreneurs don't work that way. They tend to have absolutely no idea what kind of net profits they'll have from year to year. Running a business (or many businesses!) is inherently much less predictable. Your financial decisions need to be fluid, as does the advice you're getting.

Most people who think linearly have no concept of how to manage an entrepreneur's roller-coaster situation with all the moving parts. So, what do you do to plan ahead when you don't know those concrete financial numbers? That's where this major advantage of working with an entrepreneurial advisor comes in. Figuring out how to make plans and manage that uncertainty will give you confidence as you make decisions for your business and your family.

That part about family is crucial. You've got to consider how the business finances and uncertain cash flow will affect them. As we'll discuss more in Chapter 3, entrepreneurs and their spouses or partners often have opposite personalities and mindsets toward money and risk. Typically, your spouse or significant other is not cut from the same cloth and might feel more hesitant and resistant to taking big risks and having so much uncertainty in their financial life.

I have a client whose wife has asked me many times, for example, "How much did we earn?" or "How much do you think we'll make next year? Do we have enough to do XYZ?" The entrepreneur may have no idea because there are so many potential factors that affect their business results for the year. The clearer the financial advice you receive along your entrepreneurial journey, the more prepared you'll be for whatever comes your way (and to answer some of those hard questions from the people you love). That preparation will give a lot more security and confidence to your family.

Entrepreneurial Couple Thriving, Chad and Amber in Iceland, 2023.

ABUNDANT OPPORTUNITIES EVERYWHERE

In mid-December 2023, a good friend and I were talking about the possibility of me starting a growth-coaching and leadership program for ambitious entrepreneurs (called "ELEVATED"). This conversation moved from an idea to a new business with new employees. By January 8th, less than a month later, we'd maxed out our capacity with 100 entrepreneurs already signed up for the 2024 year! The cost of this first year in the program was between $20,000 and $25,000 per person.

It's an amazing program, and our entrepreneur members are doing great things together! They're accomplishing breakthrough goals and making very valuable connections with each other. I'm absolutely loving every part of this program and feel it's an absolute blessing and a privilege to do this work. It's also true that in only three weeks, my income jumped up for the new year—just by having a brainstorming conversation, coming up with a new idea, and putting in some extra work that I really love.

When you come with an exponential mindset, everything is an opportunity.

So what does that mean for you? It's a reminder that anything is possible when you think abundantly and keep your mind open. When entrepreneurs say they don't know exactly how much they'll earn next year, that's a real answer. Maybe you're in the phase of generating possible ideas or talking with potential collaborators. When you don't have all the answers and things could go either way for you, it's tempting to mentally sit in a place of fear and scarcity: *What if it doesn't work out at all? What if our target client audience doesn't want what we're offering? What if we have great ideas and people, but the execution and follow-through doesn't get the results we want? What if our offering is priced wrong or if it costs way more than we expect from our side?*

When looking out on the year ahead as a big question mark for your expected income as an entrepreneur, I encourage my clients to put on the lens of seeing it more as an abundance of possibilities rather than as something to worry about. That's the type of wealth-generating mindset you want anyway. You could create a brand-new product line. You could create a brand-new division. You could expand into a new market. You could land the perfect deal with a collaborator who provides you with a stream of new clients who fit perfectly into your target market. All of these possibilities are real and could positively impact your bottom line.

You're an entrepreneur who's constantly looking out for what could be a new and amazing opportunity; your business and your new ideas are fluid. And that's why your financial advice must be fluid as well—because anything can happen when you approach life with an entrepreneurial mindset.

Exponential thinking is critical for success when you're an entrepreneur, and that's not what you get with an employee advisor offering traditional advice. For example, when you go to a financial advice website for retirement planning, you'll be asked to answer the same (boring) linear questions: How much can you save each month? How much money do you want to spend each month of retirement? For your trouble, you'll get an answer like this one: "If you're 45 years old and want to spend $12,000 a month when you retire at age 65, our computer program has calculated that you'll need to save $X amount for the next 20 years, allowing you to withdraw $Y when the time comes." Everything is a linear, perfect, simple, straight line.

By contrast, the entrepreneurial life looks more like a roller coaster with tons of ups and downs. If you're creative and committed, you can trust that your wealth will increase in the long run, but you've got no idea what the exact year-by-year path will look like to get there. Some years you could earn half of—or maybe double—what you earned in the previous year. Even for wage-earning employees, this kind of linear planning and forecasting is not realistic because there will always be health emergencies, downturns, unexpected family expenses, and serious inflation. In 2021 and 2022, Americans unexpectedly experienced 7–10 percent annual inflation, so how could you predict what groceries, cars, and homes will cost in thirty years? Prices are doubling almost every seven to ten years. I believe the whole linear, cookie-cutter model is very naive for everyone—but *especially* for those of you who are wired differently and reading this book.

If you have an exponential mindset, there's no ceiling to what you can earn or what you can create and grow. My coaching program was born out of nothing but an idea, and it's got real potential to be an eight-figure business in the next two years. Who knows? Nobody! And that's the fun part. When you think with an abundance mindset, believing there's plenty to go around for everyone, you keep your mind open to seeing possibilities that most people would miss.

I remember hiring a social media specialist, and I said, "We need to get our newsletter from 8,000 to 100,000 subscribers as soon as possible." They said, "Well, if we add 1,200 a month . . ." but I stopped them right there in their tracks. "I'm not looking for a steady progression of the same increment every month," I replied. "I'm aiming for exponential growth! And I know it may seem impossible, but it's not."

Countless brands have created interesting marketing campaigns and social media content that sent them skyrocketing into the spotlight. A recent example of this is GymShark, a British fitness apparel, sportswear, and accessories manufacturer and retailer based in England. In 2019, Gymshark partnered with six fitness and dance influencers on TikTok, which then led to their hashtag getting over 45.5 million views. They tried a similar viral strategy in 2020, which led to their videos and hashtag getting over 280 million views! As you can see, if you want to make a big splash as an entrepreneur, you have to think big. That's the kind of creative, flexible, ambitious planning I'm looking for. Employee advisors look at money and investing in a very incremental and linear way—a way that's unfamiliar to the creative and limitless brains of the entrepreneurs who are aiming to change the world.

Abundant world-changers are not looking to plug along at a snail's pace. A great example of that mindset is shown by well-known entrepreneur Elon Musk. His ventures SpaceX and Tesla were characterized by high risk, significant capital requirements, and long periods of illiquidity—factors that employee advisors might caution against due to their inherent risks. Elon sold his company PayPal to eBay for $1.5 billion, after which he famously said, "My personal proceeds from the PayPal acquisition were $180 million. I put $100 million in SpaceX, $70m in Tesla, and $10m in Solar City. I had to borrow money for rent." Musk's ability to weather financial uncertainty and his commitment to reinvesting all of his personal wealth into his companies underscore the entrepreneurial trait of betting big on visionary projects. He's clearly wired differently.

An employee advisor giving traditional advice would have cautioned against such concentrated risk and illiquidity, halting the groundbreaking new ideas Musk created and funded after his PayPal sale. An entrepreneurial advisor, however, would understand the value of Musk's vision, his ability to bring it to fruition, and the necessity of substantial, risky investments to revolutionize industries he was going after. Musk clearly surrounded himself with professionals who were willing to support his big dreams and entrepreneurial ideas.

"Innovation distinguishes between a leader and a follower. Entrepreneurs see opportunities where others see complexity or confusion."

–STEVE JOBS

FLUIDITY MATTERS

There's a fluidity to the advice an entrepreneur can give around cash flow that's impossible to replicate unless you've been through it yourself. In a business, cash flow is always changing. Given that fact, working with my firm includes more frequent communication than with a typical advisor, as well as answering thorough questions about the business, its financial health, and what's happening inside of it.

Based on an understanding of the fluid forces at play, an entrepreneurial advisor can give you a cash flow analysis of how and when to pay yourself. If there's a down year, they can look at the details of the situation with you and figure out whether and how much to pay out of the business. They can strategize with you to retain as much revenue as possible, rather than paying excessive taxes.

An entrepreneurial advisor will always ask questions to help you land on the right numbers specific to you and your situation. What's happening in the next six months in your business? What big expenses are you facing? How's the profitability? Do you have any plans to expand? Are you hiring? Are you laying people off? Is revenue seasonal? How's your profitability compared to last year? These are questions that often don't even ever get asked in a traditional advising firm, because—again—the advisors are so focused on the markets, the markets, the markets, and their pie charts. What entrepreneurs need advice and help on doesn't even get discussed—that is, unless you're talking to the right person.

KEY TAKEAWAYS

‣ Traditional advice for paycheck people is to keep your head down, set aside a fixed amount of money each pay period into traditional retirement vehicles, and view your balance sheet in a very black-and-white, linear way. Entrepreneurs are wired differently. They need to look at cash flow, debt, investments, and risk much differently from W-2 employees.

‣ If you're an entrepreneur who's constantly looking out for what could be a new and amazing opportunity, your business and your new ideas are fluid. That's why your financial advice must be fluid as well, because anything can happen when you approach life with exponential thinking.

‣ With an exponential mindset, there's no ceiling to what you can earn or what you can create and grow.

*"In investing,
what is comfortable
is rarely profitable."*

–ROBERT ARNOTT

CHAPTER 2

Invest in Unique Deals beyond Your Stocks and Bonds

Have you ever felt restricted by traditional financial advice? Felt like it's almost like your advisor won't give you "permission" to invest in things besides stocks and bonds? I've heard entrepreneurs complain and say, "My financial advisor always says no." Once again, that's the constraining box that frustrates entrepreneurs like you and me.

Of course, your advisor should not say yes to everything. We all know you can also blow all your money by getting overly excited about every new idea that comes across your desk. That's not my point. My point is there's a general resistance in the employee advisor industry to investment opportunities outside of your investment accounts.

One of the major unspoken reasons for this is that nearly all financial advisors are compensated based on how much money is invested in your account. On top of that, many in our industry are selling their company's own proprietary products. So when money leaves your investment account for some other opportunity—even if it's a great deal and in your best interest—your financial advisor gets a pay cut. That means advisors have actual financial incentives to keep your money where it is.

Additionally, most financial advisors have no experience personally investing in nontraditional areas. They most likely don't own multiple businesses, private stock, venture capital or private equity, cryptocurrency, or even investment real estate. It's very difficult for them to give advice on or to evaluate private investments without actual firsthand experience investing in such things. Remember, they're travel agents who have never been where you're going. You don't need a travel agent; you need a travel guide.

AN OPEN MIND AND A TWO-WAY STREET

In 2008–2009, during the big downturn, a client came to me and said, "I'm investing in this brand-new luxury real estate project, and I need to access some money from my account. Would you mind just double-checking the offering and the deal for me and telling me what you think?"

When I looked at it, I was so impressed by the opportunity that I was personally interested in investing. So I asked him if there was room for another investor, and he said he'd check with the developer. The answer was yes, and from that moment forward, I became a very committed real estate investor (during the big recession).

Prices were historically low, and nobody was buying properties. It seemed that everything was for sale. Most properties were sitting stale on the market, and banks and sellers were reducing their asking prices again and again because no offers were coming in. It was an incredible time to be a real estate investor. Because of my openness to even looking at that private deal for my client, he benefited from my review, and it also turned on a light switch for me.

My whole life changed for the better because of that opportunity. He wasn't even asking me to invest alongside him; he'd just wanted my professional advice and opinion on his potential deal. Instead of me getting fixated on him withdrawing funds from the account we managed for him and how it would impact our firm's revenue, I saw the bigger picture. The deal struck me as extremely promising, and I thought he could make a lot of money investing in that way. That's why I not only encouraged him to do it, but I also asked if I could join in. That may not sound like a big deal, but most financial advisors would simply try to discourage their clients from investing in any private real estate deals, instead focusing on keeping all their wealth in stocks and bonds.

Fast forward to today (2024): I'm invested in single-family homes, duplexes, self-storage units, apartment complexes, and commercial real estate with all kinds of different office and industrial buildings across twelve different states besides my home state of California. My wife and I invested more than $10 million in real estate during the great recession of 2007–2010, and I believe real estate can be an amazing investment that most of our clients participate in. New clients are shocked when they hear me say that, but it's true.

I love the stock market, yet I believe we should be open-minded to a wide variety of investments that provide growth and cash flow. Employee advisors typically discourage real estate for their clients, saying, "No, don't buy property. You're better off keeping all your investments in the stock market. You don't want to be a landlord anyway. You don't want to fix toilets." But guess what? That's a close-minded and shallow approach to wealth-building. And frankly, I think it's selfish of employee financial advisors to always take that stance.

You don't have to be a landlord to be a real estate investor. We're not fixing toilets, chasing down tenants for rent, or getting late night emergency calls. We've got great property managers in different states, so we don't personally touch any of those details. (If you haven't read *Who Not How* by Dan Sullivan and Dr. Benjamin Hardy yet, read that one right after you finish this book!) Robert Kiyosaki, author of *Rich Dad, Poor Dad*, is well known for advocating real estate investment as a superior alternative to the traditional brokerage investment account. His financial education programs challenge the conventional wisdom of prioritizing stocks and bonds. It's important to note that yes, historically, stocks do have a higher average annual return than real estate. However, Kiyosaki's approach demonstrates the potential for substantial wealth generation through real estate and creating other passive income streams—concepts that an entrepreneurially minded advisor would be more likely to support. Rather than take a hard stance of one asset class type versus another, I'd prefer to look at a variety of wealth-building tools for our clients (and my own family).

"It's hugely important to own investments other than traditional stocks and bonds. Traditional stocks and bonds are wonderful for diversification, and diversifying is a way to decrease risk. But there are other ways to decrease risk that I learned as an entrepreneur. Smaller businesses can be de-risked by knowing the leadership, knowing the market, understanding the business model, and being personally involved in the success of the business. Publicly traded companies don't have those to the same degree.

The largest advantage I gain from working with a wealth advisory team that understands private investments is the thought partnership. In my own business, I became very comfortable with and grew to rely on having a sparring partner or thought partner I could discuss deals with. I love to share how I'm thinking about a business or a space and see how they respond. I challenge them to challenge the investments, and then we collaborate to build comfort and conviction around each private investment."

—CASEY ADAMS,
CO-FOUNDER OF VISIBLE SUPPLY
CHAIN MANAGEMENT

NO LIMITS

When an entrepreneur says, "My financial advisor won't let me," I can't help but cringe at the missed opportunities and misaligned relationship. When my clients realize my attitude is very open to exploring new ideas together, they feel excited and inspired! Many of them never knew there were financial advisors who work holistically instead of shooting down all their innovative investing ideas.

With traditional financial advice from employee advisors, you might feel restricted and restrained. Because an entrepreneurial advisor will be open to discussing new ideas and opportunities, you get to be more creative and potentially find other ways to make more money. I've also found this type of relationship creates way more genuine loyalty and trust than if I was more motivated by keeping their money with me instead of advising on what's best for them and their family. The conflicts of interest in my industry are tough to navigate, especially when your financial advisor is not financially independent yet and in their own scarcity mode. Find an entrepreneurial advisor who is playing the abundant long-game and gives you honest and transparent feedback on the different business and investment ideas you bring to him or her.

When you're working with a fellow entrepreneur, there are endless possibilities. You can tap into your momentum and childlike excitement instead of feeling hemmed in and shot down. We're open to looking at all kinds of deals and analyzing them for our clients. Don't get me wrong: successful entrepreneurs generally don't want or need an advisor who says yes all the time, but they do want and need one who is willing to explore the opportunities for them (or together with them).

Most employee advisors aren't even willing to go there. They don't understand that when you come from an exponential creator mindset, everything's an opportunity. Shoot, they might not even be allowed (by their company's compliance department) to evaluate and give feedback on private investment or business opportunities. Nontraditional investments feel too counterintuitive and scary to someone with a scarcity mindset. An abundant-minded entrepreneur is always game to talk about different deals and new ideas. Who knows? We could be looking at the next Uber, Airbnb, or Google. How could I say no to even looking at it? That close-mindedness is a real turnoff for us as entrepreneurs; we don't like being told we can't.

ENDLESS OPTIONS

The rigid, traditional financial advice forces entrepreneurs to bake a cake with only two ingredients. These two ingredients are critical to every investor's cake, sure. Flour and butter. Stocks and bonds. But they're not including all the potential ingredients to make that cake amazingly delicious. Either way, you still get a cake, but one is very bland. Try adding some sugar, frosting, sprinkles, or fruit. The options are endless.

The most common nontraditional investments include:

- Real estate
- Private equity (investing in other private companies)
- Venture capital (investing in high risk, high potential start up companies)
- Cryptocurrency (The fact that I own Bitcoin alone definitely makes me different from many financial advisors. They won't touch it or even discuss it. I understand that people have to be very careful and consider their personal situation, but I'm open to finding ways to complement our clients' stocks and bonds.)

At the risk of being overly transparent with you, I'm sharing some of my income sources beyond stock and bond dividends and beyond my primary business, Pacific Capital:

- A coaching program (www.platinumelevated.com) for ambitious entrepreneurs
- Rent from long-term single-family homes, duplexes, apartments, and condos
- Royalties from the the four books I've written
- A sports facility that I co-founded
- A travel volleyball club and AAU basketball club that I co-founded
- Self-storage facilities
- A skilled nursing facility

- A private medical company
- A cybersecurity company
- Industrial warehouses
- Medical office complexes
- A fintech company
- A retail/multi-family complex
- Car washes
- A commercial office building
- A service company supporting financial professionals
- REITs

ILLIQUIDITY

There are opportunities in illiquid investments that you're probably not even aware of if you're working with an employee advisor. Way back when I worked at the Big Wall Street Investment Bank, we were trained to really only focus on what the firm offered to investors off the company's shelf. For many reasons, we were kept from discussing or evaluating private investment deals for clients that the firm itself didn't create.

You probably already know this, but just in case: "liquidity" is a measure of how quickly you can turn something into cash. Liquid assets can be quickly sold so that you can access the proceeds, whereas illiquid assets take a lot of time to sell to get any money back. If you have a rare art collection, for instance, it's highly illiquid. To get cash, you've got to find a buyer and agree on a price, but there's no open market for it. By contrast, you can sell stocks immediately for cash within a couple days because there's a market that's actively selling and buying. The same is true of the "cash" in your savings and checking accounts. You can use your debit card and immediately get your money out.

The only really liquid assets are in financial accounts, but entrepreneurs often have a good amount of their net worth in illiquid assets like their business. For example, if I start a restaurant and expand it to 50 locations, the value of those restaurants might be $5 million each, giving me a net worth of $250 million, but that doesn't directly translate into me having a bunch of money in my bank accounts. At that point, I have a bigtime net worth, but I may actually not have any significant cash at all. I've seen that my entire career, including some clients with a net worth over $300 million who have very low balances in their bank accounts. The bulk of an entrepreneur's net worth could be very illiquid and inaccessible at times, depending on what stage they're in.

Entrepreneurial financial advisors have a better understanding of these phases of your business and the seasons of illiquidity. An entrepreneurial advisor should have deep experience with private investments and real estate so he or she can talk to you about private and illiquid investments with confidence and expertise. They directly understand that if you invest $250,000 into a private tech company, you may need to plan on not seeing or touching that money for ten years. Even further, that company may not sell, may not distribute profits, or could go under, taking your investment to zero. It's essential to understand how illiquid investments fit into a portfolio, what role they play, and what portion of your wealth is appropriate for different types of investment categories.

An entrepreneurial advisor understands the risk and potential rewards inherent in nontraditional investments because they've got their own money in these different investment vehicles. They'll talk to you about how much money makes sense for each opportunity, or they'll tell you honestly if it's not appropriate at all for your situation. But it's an open conversation. Not everything is a home run, but an entrepreneurial financial team can do their due diligence, set you up for the best possible success, and ensure that if something doesn't work out, you still have plenty of cushion and liquidity available.

"As an entrepreneur it's important to me to align myself with other high-achieving individuals to not only learn from their experiences, but also (where possible) participate in investing in ideas and people that I believe in. My foundation for my investment philosophy will always be traditional stocks and bonds, but having the flexibility and the opportunity to invest in the success of other smaller, more entrepreneurial ventures excites me and keeps me learning and growing. Aligning with an advisory team that has experience with private investments makes me feel like they truly understand the entrepreneurial landscape and are creative in their approach to client portfolio diversification and growth. I feel like the Pacific Capital team makes clients well aware of the potential risks inherently involved in private investments, yet are aggressive (in a calculated way) in exposing their entrepreneur clientele to opportunities that fit with the risk tolerance they are accustomed to as business owners."

–JUSTIN DALTON, CEO OF CERTIFIED WASTE SOLUTIONS

YOUR NET WORTH IS YOUR NETWORK

One of our clients co-founded Quick Quack, a membership-based car wash that prides itself on being fast, fun, and affordable. It expanded until they had locations all over the western US. They decided they were going to build another 28 new car washes in California and asked if I wanted to be one of the investors. And after reviewing the financials, I said, "Absolutely, yes, I want to be a part of this—and I'd like to offer this idea to many of our clients who have an appetite for private deals." It's been a great investment because the company is led by very dynamic entrepreneurs with an appetite for growth. They have an eye for developing leaders and a great culture while scaling at an unbelievable clip.

This all may sound normal to you, but my stance is definitely unusual in our industry. By encouraging my clients to invest in other opportunities (even joining alongside them often), we're assisting them to withdraw their money *out* of the financial accounts we manage for them (removing managed assets from our firm) to help them make money on private investments we have no financial interest in. For example, there's no benefit for me if my clients chose to invest in the car wash business, but the business owners and my clients whom I connected could both benefit in a significant way. Some people would say: If I'm bringing a great deal to my clients that can make them a lot of money, but I'm also losing income by doing it, how does that make sense? Why would I do that?

Well, it makes perfect sense to me. Sure, it "lost" me money in the short term, but everyone was excited and appreciative that I connected them to a worthwhile opportunity that they couldn't have found on their own. My job is to help our clients succeed. Period. We will succeed when our clients succeed, whether that's with us or with some other deal. As this book goes to print, the investors in the car wash opportunity have been involved for less than a year, and the results have been outstanding! These clients never would've started a car wash business on their own, but I was able to connect them with an opportunity that expanded their investment portfolio.

That's one of many examples of what an entrepreneurial advisor can bring to the table when they're not constrained by a big corporate employer. There's no rigidity and nobody breathing down my neck to tell me what the bank is wanting to push and sell to the public.

Another time, we helped an out-of-state client who was looking to purchase an office building as a rental property investment. We located the broker, financially analyzed a bunch of different properties for income potential, worked with their tax advisor to make sure they were doing it in the most tax-efficient way, and helped them finance a building purchase. This client is extremely excited about the great cash flow that's coming from that opportunity—and especially appreciative that he didn't have to do much in the process.

Part of what an entrepreneurial advisor will offer is ensuring that you minimize your fees and costs on all these outside, private deal opportunities. Because we're looking out for you (our clients) and because we have no "skin in the game" as your fiduciaries, we don't get paid from any of these outside deals. We simply represent your best interest at all times. That's why we review the contracts and try to ensure that you get the best possible treatment in terms. Entrepreneurs appreciate that depth and level of service because we'll catch things in a contract or an offering and say, "Hey, we think you should negotiate and ask for something better. Here's what we've seen in other similar deals or offerings." That adds an extra layer of support and insight as clients are navigating different opportunities that come across their desks. If they were looking at everything on their own, it just wouldn't be as effective. We've looked at so many thousands of deals and contracts that we know how to quickly identify problems—and, of course, opportunities.

If you're thinking, "But wait, isn't financial advice financial advice either way? Wouldn't everyone know how to examine contracts and terms of different private investments or real estate deals?" The answer is no.

No matter how much it seems like we're interchangeable, employee advisors who work for big banks and insurance companies are in a different sandbox regarding how they're trained, what they're exposed to, and even how they get paid. I'm not suggesting there's a good side and dark side in our industry. But there certainly are distinct differences, and most people just simply have no idea. Employee advisors who work for these brokerage firms, big banks, and insurance companies are constrained by different policies and incentives that favor their employer. They may have many layers of middle management above them and less open architecture because their offerings are solely based on who their employer has deals or agreements with. The system is just set up that way. They can make more money by recommending you (their clients) invest in Fund A versus Fund B, even if Fund B would be better for you—or maybe you shouldn't be looking at a fund at all.

Our approach is way more relational and less transactional than at a big commission-based bank. As an entrepreneur and a fiduciary, I want nothing more than for my clients to win.

KEY TAKEAWAYS

‣ Most financial advisors have no (or very little) experience personally investing in nontraditional areas. They most likely don't own multiple businesses, private stock, venture capital, private equity, cryptocurrency, or even investment real estate. It's very difficult for them to give advice on or to evaluate private investments without actual firsthand experience investing in such things. Remember, they're travel agents who have never been where you're going. You don't need a travel agent, you need a travel *guide*.

‣ With traditional financial advice from employee advisors, you might feel restricted and restrained. Because an entrepreneurial advisor will be open to discussing new ideas and opportunities, you get to be more creative and potentially find other ways to make more money. Entrepreneurial financial advisors also have a better understanding of the phases of your business and the seasons of illiquidity.

‣ By encouraging clients to invest in other opportunities (even joining alongside them often), an entrepreneurial advisor can assist you in withdrawing your money out of the financial accounts they manage for you (removing managed assets) to help *you* make money on private investments *they* have no financial interest in.

*"Leadership is not about being in charge.
It's about taking care of those in your charge.
In a family business, this means not just looking
after the business, but the family itself."*

–SIMON SINEK

CHAPTER 3

Strengthen Your Family with Entrepreneurship

If you think entrepreneurs feel misunderstood, the entrepreneurial couple is its own animal. Entrepreneurial couples generally include someone who's very comfortable with uncertainty and risks and who might even love taking big chances . . . paired with someone who's the complete opposite. This is usually someone who likes to plan ahead, favors security, and seeks knowing the potential downside or the outcomes if things don't go their way.

This difference in your risk comfort level often creates conflict in your relationship. One of you quickly pursues new ideas full-throttle, while the other slams on the brakes and wants to talk about all the what-ifs of the new idea or new investment. Having an entrepreneurial advisor who understands entrepreneurial couples offers an important source of mediation to get you and your partner more aligned. That alignment leads to greater harmony and financial success because both of your needs are being met.

Now, don't get me wrong, there's great value in opposites attracting. One of my favorite comedians, Nate Bargatze, talks about how "you can't have two dreamers in a marriage." He says, "You need to have one person who hates fun, because if you have two dreamers, you'll be homeless in an hour. One person needs to walk around asking, 'Is there fun happening here? I'm going to put a stop to that.'" That's obviously a bit exaggerated, but there's truth in it.

This dynamic plays out in my own relationship. My wife comes from a mindset and perspective that's more financially conservative, so she's very risk-averse. She often gets nervous about the new things we're getting into, asking, "How are you going to make this happen?" and, "What if it doesn't work out?" Where I might see no problem or reason to worry (because I'm sure it will all *somehow* work out), she feels unsettled. This is actually a good balance and keeps me in check, but it can be frustrating when I'm trying to push the pedal of the Ferrari all the way to the floor while she's trying to pull up the emergency brakes so we can first "talk through the idea first."

I've been married for 23 years, so I personally understand the issues and challenges at play when I'm counseling with entrepreneurial couples. Tension and conflict around money and business decisions can really be an obstacle for many families. New clients often seem pleasantly surprised to hear that they're not alone in this roller coaster of life as an entrepreneurial couple, and they're often more at ease when I can share ideas and solutions from my own life experience with them.

Chad & Amber in Hawaii, Thanksgiving, 2023.

GETTING ALIGNED

My wife and I recently went to a marriage retreat that wasn't what you'd traditionally expect. It was very specifically framed for entrepreneurial couples, where one spouse tends to be a wild dreamer. We found the content and exercises to be very interesting and insightful. The main takeaway lessons weren't that we need to agree about everything. Instead, they were that we need to be aligned and to increase our communication in order to get there . . . together. Marriage and long-term relationships are tough enough as it is, so when you add in the roller coaster ride of being married to an entrepreneur, you're dumping fuel on that fire! At that retreat, we wrote down our big goals and dreams for us individually, as a couple, and then as a family, regarding what we think is possible in the next five and ten years. The exercise was inspiring and connecting.

Chad and Amber at an Entrepreneurial Couple
Marriage Retreat in Florida, 2023.

At a regular marriage retreat, we might have encountered much more linear thinking and traditional planning that didn't feel tailored to us. The counsel wouldn't have incorporated all the nuances of being on the entrepreneurial journey together. It would've lacked exponential thinking, and we would've felt out of place there. Instead, we were surrounded by couples who all go through the same struggles that my wife and I do. It was so healthy and refreshing to hear other couples facing almost the same communication issues that we've dealt with in our 23 years of marriage. It turns out we aren't that different from this subset of the population.

As an entrepreneur, maybe you've had the common experience of getting frustrated because you feel like you can't even talk to your partner about all your big new ideas. You anticipate the fire being put out before you can even get it started, with comments like, "No, we can't do that. I don't see how that could work." Or, "We can't afford that." After that happens a few times, you might start withholding information or excitement around your new ideas from your spouse.

In truth, what an uncertain partner really needs in that situation is a sense of security, reassurance, and a plan. They need to see the numbers. They don't want to rely on optimism and visions alone.

Of course, both sides have good intentions, but you need to find a better way to communicate. That's one thing we've really worked on as we've attended the entrepreneurial couples retreat two years in a row now. Entrepreneurial couples are usually aligned in their big goals and family values, but they don't always agree on how to get there. So they either just don't talk about it, which is not great, or they have lots of tension and conflict because they're not speaking the same language. They could both look at the same idea and see something totally different as the potential outcome.

One of our clients recently called me and said, "I'm super frustrated. My wife wants all this data and planning info about our finances, and she can't see the opportunity of what I'm trying to do. She thinks we can't afford it and doesn't understand what this opportunity actually could bring to us." They had just sold their business. He was starting something new, and she felt very nervous. They had no paycheck coming in. They had a very large investment account, but no regular paycheck from a company. The truth was they definitely *could* afford it, but she was simply more prone to worry about financial security and where their cash flow would be coming from.

I said, "Don't worry about this—let me talk to her. I know exactly how to help here." He said I'd be his hero if I could explain it in some way that would help her feel secure and stable. I got on the phone with her and said, "Tell me what you're concerned about."

"Well, he wants to start this thing, and it's going to take a chunk of our money up front. And he's got other investment ideas he's looking at . . . what if it doesn't work out? Where's our future income going to come from?" she asked. "We already sold the business, and our paycheck deposits have stopped coming in."

(By the way, this is common. We specialize in working with people who sell their businesses and have walked so many families through this phase of business and life. It's an understandably important emotional transition, when you go from someone with high cash flow to someone with a large bank account and no direct deposit coming in.)

I talked her through the numbers, showed her where they stood financially, and gave her reassurance of guardrails on how much they could safely invest in new projects and ideas. We put an upper limit on what would be financially advisable to invest in the new venture. I told her I thought it would work out, but even if it didn't, they'd still be okay. They had all these other assets to rely on.

I communicated with her in a way about their family's financial plan that her husband just couldn't because I understand *both sides* of what they're feeling. He (as the visionary entrepreneur) needed room to think about the big possibilities and new opportunities for growth while also getting some advice on the risks, and she (as the responsible planner who is more risk-averse) needed the concrete information and data to feel more secure. Neither approach is right or wrong in those black and white terms, but speaking to both approaches in a different language was key for them to move forward as an aligned couple. An entrepreneurial advisor

"Chad and his team approach wealth management differently than any financial advisor I've ever met. It's the difference between someone talking to you and talking at you. Plus, it's so much more fun and exciting when you work with people who think like you do and who understand what that means in the big picture."

–CHAD JOHNSON, ENTREPRENEUR AND BUSINESS COACH

will understand how to do that. If you're being advised or coached by someone without personal experience in these issues, neither of you will feel fully understood.

ALONG FOR THE ROLLER COASTER RIDE

The dynamics in an entrepreneurial family are fundamentally different from those in other families. The non-entrepreneurs in the family are on a roller coaster ride (or at least have a front row seat to watch the ride) that most people don't understand. They're being tossed and turned and pulled and yanked in all these different directions. It can be very scary for them.

When I left Merrill Lynch, my wife and I had just bought a large house in Southern California. When we bought the big house, I was 30 years old, she was 27, and it was during what's now known as "The Great Recession." We had three kids, including a new baby boy. I'd been making seven figures in a very comfortable corporate job, but I decided I wanted to leave the Big Wall Street Bank and basically start all over again, this time as an entrepreneur. My wife's response was, "Are you serious right now? We just moved, have a big mortgage with a lot of expenses coming up. With three kids and more on the way"—she was right, we ended up with five kids—"it seems like a risky time to let go of that income and start over. What if it doesn't work out? What will you do then? You can't go back to your old job once you leave. I'm not sure about this. It sounds very risky."

I optimistically replied, "I'll make it work out. Don't worry about it. I'm gonna do everything I can to make sure we succeed. I've got to do this. I can't work there anymore." I felt confident, but I didn't have any guarantees of security that could demonstrate to her how it would work. Thankfully, it definitely did work out for the best, and I've never looked back with regret once. Still, it's hard to share and communicate the vision when you have a different mindset and when you're speaking a different language. You're simply wired differently. That's why it's so valuable to get family and financial advice from people who have walked in your shoes and completely get what you're going through. An entrepreneurial advisor knows firsthand what your family is going through when you're making big decisions like selling a company, starting a company, moving across the country, or taking a big investment risk. There's a lot at stake! Having that support in your corner changes how you approach your decision-making and communication in the family.

CONSIDERING THE NEXT GENERATION

Many entrepreneurs have a vision of their kids working for or taking over the family business. Some of the challenges you face in a family business include:

- Family governance and decision-making
- Conflict resolution
- Succession and legacy planning
- Family charitable giving and philanthropy
- Family involvement and compensation

The Willardson family in Sundance, Utah, 2023.

These are all important considerations if you're running a family business, and an employee advisor traditionally won't have much (if any) experience on those counts. You need to consider how to balance professionalism and standards with family culture and values. There are emotional dynamics too, including the attachment family members feel to the business and to each other, which can influence the financial decisions you're facing.

When counseling entrepreneurs, financial advisors need to be mindful of these emotional dynamics and provide advice that considers the well-being of the family alongside the financial health of the business. If the goal of the business is to leave a lasting legacy, which I'll talk about more in Chapter 6, then you need someone who understands your values and goals as well as how to balance them with the next generation's vision and desires. It's a delicate dance. (P.S. I'm not just casually interested in this topic. I wrote the book *Smart, Not Spoiled* and am the co-host of the *Smart Money Parenting* show. The financial literacy of the next generation is very important to me—for my kids and for yours. We'll talk more about that soon.)

You also need to consider how to integrate non-family executives into the leadership team without causing resentment or diminishing your family's control or influence. Wealth advisors often have to play a mediator role, helping to resolve conflicts in a way that protects both the business's interests and the family relationships. Personal and professional disagreements may sometimes collide with business and finances. It's particularly challenging when you don't have a third party to assist in mediating conflict resolution.

Businesses that get passed down for generations can often grow into something very significant. We work with an agribusiness that has been around for 80 years and 4 generations. The clients grew the business like crazy in the last two decades—from a $20 million dollar value to over a $300 million dollar value. Their adult children are very involved in running the company and own over 40 percent of it. The next generation of family members in their business has ambitious goals to invest in growth assets and new technology, while the older generation is nearing retirement and would love to be compensated for the decades of growth in sweat equity. There's definitely some tension between what the next generation wants and the older generations' retirement plans.

This is complex, and there are many implications of ownership, estate planning, tax planning, etc. It's going to take a lot of strategy and scenario planning to help all parties get what they want out of the next five years in this family business. You need someone who understands these sensitive dynamics at play, much more than being able to run an online retirement planning calculator or silly pie chart on a slide deck. Even if you've thought to ask your employee advisor about these issues, what can they advise in this situation? How would they not have a limited perspective, having never been an entrepreneur themselves? What's their advice going to be based on for running a business that involves family members if they work for a big corporate bank or an insurance company?

An entrepreneurial advisor should understand some of the family dynamics involved when running a business. My parents were not entrepreneurs, so I didn't learn these things as a kid. (For the record,

Chad with his parents, Craig and Betsy Willardson,
at their home in Orange County, CA.

I did learn every other valuable lesson about work ethic, integrity, character, and success from Mom and Dad. Thank you.) But I *have* been on the journey with my own wife and five kids, the oldest of whom will turn 20 this year. Each of the kids has been hired to do work for our different companies at different times. When they were much younger, my kids would come to the office to do intern work, scan, shred, clean, or even participate in my marketing video recordings. My family members are on our payroll, and I enjoy involving them in the work that we do. So when clients have questions about their family business or how they can involve their kids in their company, I can speak to them from personal experience. I can say with honesty, "Here's how I look at incorporating my family members into business activities and how I've tried to balance personal family relationships with business and financial matters."

"Entrepreneurial families are unique. They have many needs that only entrepreneurs can really relate to. And it's such an advantage for these families to be mentored and counseled by those who understand what it's like to be an entrepreneurial family."

—SHANNON WALLER, COACH & DIRECTOR AT STRATEGIC COACH®

Decision-making in a family business needs to honor the goals and roles of the different stakeholders in the family. They'll be different ages and in different financial circumstances, so their approach and view of the family business and finances will often conflict with each other. I've seen some very difficult situations when family members have equal pay or equal ownership amounts but exert very unequal levels of effort. That's why you also need to ensure you have the right people in the right seats, looking at the different talents, skills, commitment levels, and interests of the family to determine how they can best be utilized inside your business. You can promote education and growth, empowering family members and fostering a sense of ownership of and commitment to the business's success.

TEACHING FINANCIAL LITERACY

Financial literacy for kids is an important consideration. (As I mentioned earlier, for more on this subject, I invite you to read *Smart, Not Spoiled,* check out *Value Creation Kid,* and listen to the *Smart Money Parenting* podcast.) In a nutshell: done right, hiring your kids serves as hands-on business and wealth education for the next generation. Through your endeavors, you can help teach business and money skills to the younger people in your family and set them up to be successful and prepared adults someday.

Support for the family dynamics (and its accompanying challenges) of entrepreneurship is relevant whether or not you plan to pass the business down to future generations. You could have plans to sell it as an exit strategy, but there are still a lot of family considerations if you sell your business. How much will each person get? Will any ownership be retained? Who still might be working in the business after a sale? Are there any family members who used to work in the business but don't any longer who might have a say in the sale, etc.? Will the medical benefits and other business-paid perks be lost for certain family members who really need it if the business ownership is sold or transferred to someone outside of the family? When you run a business, you've got lots of potential stakeholders and families to consider, from the boardroom to your living room, who will all be affected by your business financial decisions.

However, if you're a W-2 employee advisor at a big company, you don't have those same issues. You work at a job, and get your paycheck from said job, but it kind of ends with that. Your family doesn't have to be super involved and may not be affected regardless of what positions you have at work or if you change from one company to another. That's vastly different from being a business owner who employs your spouse, kids, or other relatives. Family businesses are not like typical day jobs.

I always say *"more is caught than taught"* when it comes to parenting. This plays out all around us if we're paying attention. You often pick up a lot of your viewpoints of the world through the lens of your childhood. Whatever is being modeled in your home when you're a child is what you believe is "normal." For example, I'm always inspired by stories of people with big dreams and resilience who pass those things onto their kids through what they *do*, not just what they say. Consider the struggle and perseverance of many immigrants who come to the US with nothing, and because they have no other choice, they hustle and turn their life into something spectacular. Many of them are desperate to create a better life for their families, and they'll do whatever it takes to survive (and then eventually, thrive). And their kids grow up learning how to work hard and grind, helping out in the family store, laundromat, or whatever small business their parents started here in the US. Often, these children of immigrants become phenomenal entrepreneurs because that simple enterprise and hustle their parents modeled out of desperation served them like a "business school degree" (probably even more than a business school degree would have) to make them successful entrepreneurs. A great example of this are my clients and friends Andy, Tony, and Juan Dominguez, whose family escaped Cuba years ago. They were threatened by the government and lost everything. When they got to the US, Andy's father started his own business. Today, all of the Dominguez children are successful, and most of them are business owners themselves. I have great respect for that whole family.

If you're an entrepreneur fortunate enough to also be a parent, just know that your children are watching you, your work ethic, your attitude toward work and money, and even how you run your business and talk about your employees. They're soaking it all up. Every day, they see you embody what it means to put your family's entire financial future on your back and carry it forward with confidence, despite the uncertainty in life. They absorb that mentality you bring and are more likely to apply it to their own lives and financial futures when they get older.

It's also true that part of the entrepreneurial spirit is leaning into your strengths. Maybe running a business is not your child's strength and they won't take your company over from you . . . which is fine! I don't believe all five of our kids will choose this life of entrepreneurship, and I'm certain a few of them wouldn't be attracted to wealth management, coaching, or writing like me. But my kids and your kids will still learn and absorb a lot from the example we set as entrepreneurial parents: innovating, solving problems for others, dealing with customers, approaching potential customers, leading with emotional intelligence, handling complaints or a bad review on Yelp or Google, pivoting to a new idea or market, balancing the money coming in and out, navigating what happens in the economy . . . the list goes on. One of the coolest lessons my kids got to witness was the struggle I went through as an early entrepreneur. Then, over a decade later, they came on stage with me as I won an "Entrepreneur of the Year" award in Southern California.

*Chad and his family when Chad won an Entrepreneur
of the Year Award in 2021 in Southern CA.*

Another great entrepreneurial observation time period for my kids
was during the COVID pandemic. It's important for kids in entrepreneurial families to see how to react when massive, unexpected
disruption happens. The economy came to a screeching halt, the
investment markets dropped 40 percent in less than 6 weeks, and
people everywhere were panicked. What did your kids and family
members observe from you? Did they see a lot of fear? Was it your
steady resolve? Did they see you innovate and create or completely
pivot altogether? For my sports business, we went from hosting
thousands of kids and families for tournaments and practices to
absolutely nothing. A massive, empty sports facility in Southern
California with no end in sight.

After many months of my business partners and I trying to find
ways to earn money and stay within the California rules of no
gathering, we found a different use and opportunity for our sports
facility. There was a state law at the time that allowed for gathering

Chad's sports complex facility in Southern CA.

for "remote learning students who are children of 'essential workers.'"
So we decided to convert our big gym into a place where essential
workers could have their kids do their online school work during
the day (under supervision from tutors we hired) while they worked
at the hospitals or other places that required people to be in person.
My kids saw us buying hundreds of desks and supplies to convert
the gym into a tutoring center. This move kept a steady stream of

revenue coming in and saved us from losing the business and millions of dollars. No matter what kind of career my kids choose someday, that's a lesson they'll never forget. And neither will I.

Success requires everyone involved in the business to have a basic level of personal financial competency and education. They need a sense of how their work contributes to the business, and they need to be personally responsible and financially stable if they're going to be entrusted with making the *business* profitable, stable, and growing. Your business can and should be an extension of your family values. You can teach your family to be smart, not spoiled and how to use wealth in a way that leaves a positive impact and a legacy.

ROLE MODELS

Do Won Chang and his wife, Jin Sook Chang, immigrated from South Korea with no college education, no money, and no fluency in English. They worked as a janitor and a gas station attendant, and then in 1984, they opened a small clothing store with hopes that they could sell a few items of clothes. Maybe you've heard of their store? It's called Forever 21. I love their example of grinding out a tough job and then deciding to go for something big.

Another great entrepreneurial family we can all learn from is that of Sara Blakely and Jesse Itzler. If you don't already know, Sara founded Spanx. Her journey is an interesting one: she'd planned to become an attorney, but that didn't pan out. She began selling fax machines door to door and quickly ascended the ranks, excelling in sales. But she didn't like being forced to wear pantyhose, so she set out to develop a product that would achieve the same result without the discomfort. She spent years and much of her savings account developing the concept before presenting it to representatives from many of America's hosiery mills. They turned her down—except for one, who had been encouraged by his daughters that the concept was strong. Further inspired and energized, Sara filed for a patent and purchased the trademark for her new company, Spanx, which she eventually sold for over $1 billion. She ultimately gave million-dollar bonuses to every single employee who started with her, making them all instant millionaires.

Her husband Jesse is also an incredible inspiration of hustle and innovation. Jesse hustled from nothing, just working in coffee shops and trying to sell stuff on the side as a misfit kid and wannabe rapper. He worked from the ground up to create a pretty dynamic business resume: Jesse is the co-founder of Marquis Jet (one of the largest private jet membership companies in the world), a partner in Zico Coconut Water, the founder of The 100 Mile Group, and one of the owners of the NBA's Atlanta Hawks.

If you haven't heard all of Jesse's story, you're going to want to: he wrote the book *Living with a SEAL* about David Goggins. Jesse invited him to come live with his family and tell him all about his life. After he'd already extended the invite and David accepted it, Jesse went home and told Sara he'd invited this stranger to come live with them and their young kids for a month. It changed all of their lives. Goggins went on to write his own book and become a *New York Times* bestselling author, all because Jesse saw him next to his tent at the race.

My wife and I first heard Jesse speak eight years ago. It was electric. He got so passionate about sharing how it seemed, for a time, like he was not going to make it and would end up a total failure. He was trying this, trying that, just hustling on the streets—and then he got a break. Somehow, he scrapped his way to being successful, and that success grew and grew and grew. I've since met and talked with him a few times at different events, and I'm always more impressed than the previous time.

Sara and Jesse are a great couple and a great example of how understanding the family dynamics of entrepreneurship by supporting each other can result in amazing things. Imagine what their four kids have seen and experienced and how they'll approach their life decisions differently than most. These young kids have seen each of their parents take a very unique path to business and life. They can see that mom and dad are most definitely wired differently!

Chad Willardson, Jesse Itzler, and Justin Lyon.

KEY TAKEAWAYS

‣ Traditional employee advisors might separate personal finance from business finance, overlooking the synergy and support systems that family can provide. By contrast, an entrepreneurial advisor isn't just there to navigate conflict but also to help you and your family support each other and leverage the value that support can bring.

‣ Having an entrepreneurial advisor who understands entrepreneurial couples offers an important source of mediation to get you and your partner more aligned. That alignment leads to greater harmony and financial success because both of your needs are being met.

‣ Support for the family dynamics of entrepreneurship is relevant whether or not you plan to pass the business down. You could aim to sell it, but there are still family relationships to attend to in the process. When you run a business, you have multiple stakeholders to consider, from the boardroom to your living room, who will be affected by your financial decisions.

"If you're not leveraging the balance sheet, you're walking on one leg. Smart investors know how to balance risk and reward across assets and liabilities."

—RAY DALIO

CHAPTER 4

Leverage Both Sides of Your Balance Sheet

As an entrepreneurial advisor, I believe in creatively looking at both sides of the balance sheet—assets and liabilities—as opportunities for growth.

That puts me at odds with celebrity money experts like Dave Ramsey and Suze Orman who very successfully sell courses worldwide about personal finance. Ramsey, for example, has written that "the truth about debt" is "it's a wrecking ball, both to your money and your mental health." He says people "who want you to believe debt is a tool you can use to build wealth . . . are plain wrong. Your biggest wealth-building tool is actually your income."[1]

---

1 David Ramsey, "The Truth about Debt," Ramsey, Feb. 10, 2023, https://www.ramseysolutions.com/debt/the-truth-about-debt.

Well, when it comes to entrepreneurs, I think his advice is plain wrong. In our exponential context of thinking big and outside the box, I disagree that all debt is bad debt and that you need to be debt-free to achieve financial success. I feel it's important to make that distinction because savvy entrepreneurs, especially those who are building wealth, use debt and leverage to their advantage. They use both sides of the balance sheet to grow wealth.

Most traditional employee advisors have a very black-and-white view of assets and liabilities. They might echo the sentiment that assets are good and liabilities are bad. By contrast, Robert Kiyosaki, author of *Rich Dad, Poor Dad*, is a major advocate of using debt to build wealth. He talks about how your primary residence is actually a liability. It's not an asset, because it costs money and doesn't produce any cash flow for you. Does that mean you shouldn't buy a house? Of course not! But it's definitely a different way of looking at your home.

Traditional financial advice will often discourage debt completely, seeing it as something too risky or imprudent on your wealth-building journey, because typical employee advisors see the financial path toward "retirement" as linear. They think you should build up a little wealth with each paycheck and pay down a little debt until the wealth is at least to the number you want . . . and the debt is finally zero.

But an entrepreneurial, exponential mindset looks at the whole sum of the opportunity, which will not always be paid in cash up front. Some of it will be financed. This is especially smart when rates are low and inflation is rising (you'll be able to buy assets with today's dollars and pay back loans with future, less valuable dollars). If you're working with a linear, anti-debt advisor as an entrepreneur, you're not going to get the same advice. The risk comfort level is going to be low, and you'll be encouraged to take the safe route. As a result, you'll miss the opportunities outside of your cash affordability range, which is usually where all the big future growth is. Let me repeat that for you: the biggest growth happens outside of what you've already accomplished or what you can currently afford with cash.

An entrepreneurial advisor will look at strategic use of debt as an opportunity builder. It's like finding a bank that can be a business partner in your venture, which is often necessary. You often can't just pay for your idea or an opportunity upfront—it's too expensive. If you wait until you can afford everything in cash, you might end up being old and gray and still waiting.

HOW I USED DEBT TO BUILD WEALTH

When I got into real estate investing during the 2008–2009 US recession, I did so because home prices had dropped dramatically. Plus, it seemed everyone was pessimistic about the future of America . . . and especially real estate in America. Banks were panicking, homeowners were panicking, and there were short sales and bank foreclosures everywhere. It was a complete fire sale. In case you forgot, home prices dropped between 35 percent and 40 percent on average during that time period. Many homeowners and banks were selling for 50 percent below what the value was a year prior. Banks desperately wanted to get these houses off their balance sheets because they had so much negative equity on the books. I bought a couple rental properties for deep discounts. It almost didn't seem real that they were going for such a discount when the cash flow from rents was so good. Because I didn't have a ton more cash sitting around to pay for more, I decided to find banks that would partner with me in this new venture based on my financial creditworthiness and my business plan to build a big real estate portfolio. Had I not engaged in borrowing money for those investment ideas, I never would've been able to build the portfolio that I've built.

I borrowed and bought until I had ten new mortgages. At the time, banks had a limit of ten mortgages per person. Once I maxed out that limit, all the banks said, "Sorry, that's enough. You're done, Chad." But I wasn't done! I could still see all these opportunities out there and wasn't willing to just let them pass by. I needed to jump on them. No one was buying houses at the time, but I knew the markets would turn around someday. So I took Mr. Warren Buffett's sage advice: "Be greedy when others are fearful and fearful when others are greedy."

I found a commercial bank that would do one large business loan and pay off all ten mortgages, wrapping them up under one umbrella loan covering all the houses at once. Now I was back to only one mortgage and could get nine more, which I did. I did that a few times. Meanwhile, we were able to use the cash flow from rents to pay down and pay off some of the properties.

Based on that successful experience of building a solid base of assets and so many others while working with our clients, I can say with confidence that debt is just not black and white. I never would have amassed a few dozen income-generating properties during that recession if I wasn't willing to take a risk and use some debt. Because of that experience as an entrepreneur and investor, we look at debt in a creative way to help our clients drive growth where we see opportunities.

Some entrepreneurs come to us only ever having heard from financial advisors that debt is bad and should be avoided or paid down as fast as possible. That's when we explain our philosophy of why you benefit from staying open-minded when looking at *both* sides of your balance sheet. So much of that open mindset toward more creative wealth-building strategies goes back to that exponential, opportunity orientation rather than a rigid, linear mindset toward financial planning.

USE DEBT TO EXPAND YOUR EXISTING BUSINESS

Debt isn't only for new opportunities, like getting into real estate or buying into someone else's startup. Sometimes it makes sense to take on debt to reinvest for your own growth, rather than looking externally. Borrowing capital allows you to invest in your business expansion opportunities, inventory, marketing, or new product development.

An entrepreneurial advisor should advise using loans strategically in your business. For example, I used the Small Business Administration (SBA) to get very good terms on financing for the building I purchased to serve as the new Pacific Capital headquarters, slated to open this year near one of our current locations in Southern California. The SBA is there precisely to help entrepreneurs like us finance our growth.

Debt is a much cheaper form of capital compared to giving up equity in your business. Say you start a family restaurant business, and you need $100,000 to buy a huge oven and quality equipment for the big kitchen. You can go to a bank or credit union and ask, "Can I borrow $100,000 and pay it back over ten or twenty years?" Or you can go to your friend or neighbor to ask for the $100,000, but they might say, "Sure, but I want 50 percent of your company." That's a very expensive form of capital because now that neighbor owns half your company. They get half of any profits you make for the rest of your life.

"The balance sheet is the foundation of a business. Wise entrepreneurs and investors understand that managing both sides efficiently is the key to long-term success."

—WARREN BUFFETT

By contrast, if you're borrowing money from the bank, you just have to pay the bank back the money you borrowed plus some interest every year, and then you're done with it. You still own 100 percent of your creation, so all the money you make and the equity value you build from the restaurant is yours forever. Raising capital is expensive. Giving up ownership early in your journey is tough because you won't get it back. Borrowing allows you to keep your ownership.

USE DEBT TO SEIZE OPPORTUNITIES IN
FAST-MOVING MARKETS

In fast-moving markets or tumultuous economic seasons, the ability to quickly seize opportunities can be a significant competitive advantage. Debt can provide the immediate capital necessary to capitalize on these opportunities.

We have a client in the private at-home-care business, caretaking elderly and disabled people who need help. We've worked with him to find creative finance opportunities that would allow him to buy smaller, more mom-and-pop home-care companies that come up for sale, allowing him to grow his company more and more. Besides creative financing, we're also there for thought partnership around big-picture considerations like timing and overall strategy. Because we're experienced as entrepreneurs *and* wealth managers, we're also able to advise and counsel the entrepreneurs *on the other side* of our client's deals, too. Often, this is the first time they'll have ever sold a business, so they have a lot of questions about what's next and how to best plan their transition from busy business owner/operator to someone with a very large bank account and a new life outside of their business. Being able to help on both ends of these transactions not only expands our impact, but it also gives our clients higher likelihoods of success in getting deals closed because all parties feel heard and professionally supported.

Typically the owners of these small businesses my client is acquiring don't want a lengthy and complex process; they simply want an opportunity to retire while taking care of their long-term employees

Wealth Wired Differently

at their business. Maybe their asking price is $30 million for their business, but if they could cash out and get paid in less than a week or two, they'd take $25 million! After making an agreement like that, our client will call us to access a loan against his portfolio, and *boom*, he has the $25 million and buys another company to roll up into his business. If he didn't have quick access to capital, that kind of acquisition would be a longer and slower process. With the support of an entrepreneurial advisory team, he can jump on good deals and stay in growth mode.

There are other benefits to strategically using debt as well. It can help you build a business credit history, which can be advantageous for securing larger loans or lines of credit in the future—and with more favorable terms. This can facilitate continued growth and expansion opportunities for your business.

Entrepreneurs also often use debt to fund innovation and experimentation within their business, which might not provide immediate returns but are crucial for long-term growth and adaptation. This willingness to invest in unproven areas can lead to breakthroughs that significantly enhance your business's value down the line.

NOT INHERENTLY GOOD OR BAD

Debt isn't *necessarily* good or bad. There is bad debt. There is good debt. There are no hard-and-fast standards about how much to have or what makes debt inherently bad or good; it depends on your particular circumstances, what the debt will be used for, what

86

other money is accessible to you, and the loan terms you're given. Honestly, there are no rules of thumb that apply every time in every case. Nothing is universally applicable, because the details are individual. Any financial advisor giving the same blanket advice to every client about debt isn't using a creative, entrepreneurial, exponential mindset.

Daymond John has often discussed the strategic use of debt and growing his business. He used debt to grow FUBU, and his investments in private businesses on the hit TV show *Shark Tank* that often include offers for creative loans illustrate a nuanced understanding about leveraging financial tools to build a business.

Your strategic advisors should be helping you look at your financial life holistically, considering current interest rates and inflation, and with an awareness of what's happening around you in the business world and in your industry. That context gives you a better sense of when it's more advantageous to use debt or not.

For example, when I was actively buying real estate, I was finding mortgage rates barely over 3 percent. With interest rates, inflation, and real estate values expected to jump over the next decade, it made a lot of sense for me to borrow cheap money to invest in assets that would appreciate at much more than 3 percent per year. On top of that, with inflation increasing, I knew I'd be paying the loan off (or more accurately, our tenants would be) with cheaper-valued dollars in the future. If you want to get *really* technical, that capital was not actually costing me 3 percent per year because of the tax deductibility of the loan interest. So it may have been closer to 1.5 to 2 percent annually while the asset value eventually increased at 15 to 20 percent per year. In that environment, it actually made sense to borrow as much money as I could possibly get my hands on and make a great profit on someone else's capital. (Using the bank's money to buy an asset that increased double digits nearly every year with increasing rental cash flow each year was a no-brainer.) If someone is willing to give you one dollar that you can eventually turn into two, and you've only got to pay back a few cents of interest, how much money would you want them to give you?

If you understand inflation, interest rates, business and investment opportunities, and where we are in the economic cycles, why would you eliminate all options to use debt in your financial strategies . . . just because your grandparents and their financial guy says all debt is bad? That doesn't make much sense. You should at least have great strategic conversations with entrepreneurial advisors to look at all options on the table for raising capital.

Debt's goodness or badness depends on your circumstances as well as the broader business and economic environment. That's the value of you working with an entrepreneurial advisory team who can really help you explore both sides of your balance sheet—and, as I'll explain in the next chapter, help legally reduce your tax liabilities, too.

KEY TAKEAWAYS

▸ Most traditional employee advisors have a very black-and-white view of assets and liabilities. But an entrepreneurial, exponential mindset looks at the whole sum of the opportunity and sees the value of leveraging both sides of the balance sheet. In other words, some things need to be financed. If you're working with a linear, anti-debt advisor as an entrepreneur, you're missing the opportunities outside of your affordability range, which is usually where all the growth is. The biggest growth happens outside of what you've already accomplished or what you can currently afford with cash.

▸ Debt isn't only for new opportunities, like getting into real estate or staking someone else's startup. Sometimes it makes sense to take on debt to reinvest for your own growth, rather than looking externally. By borrowing capital, you can invest in expansion opportunities, inventory, marketing, or new product development without diluting your equity.

▸ In fast-moving markets, the ability to quickly seize opportunities can be a significant competitive advantage. Debt can provide the immediate capital necessary to capitalize on these opportunities—something an entrepreneurial advisor will be naturally inclined to notice.

"I am proud to be paying taxes in the United States. The only thing is—I could be just as proud for half the money."

–ARTHUR GODFREY

CHAPTER 5

Get Proactive Tax Advice and Strategy

That's a funny quote, but can you argue with it? You've heard your entire life as an entrepreneur that it's not about what you make, it's about what you keep. As a startup entrepreneur, you have very different concerns and headaches than an established peer who's got many businesses firing on all cylinders. But one thing we've all got in common is our desire to really maximize the value and impact of every dollar that comes in the door of our business. The sooner you learn the difference between proactive and reactive in your business financial planning, the sooner you'll understand how important entrepreneurial strategic advisors are to your life. Most entrepreneurs come to us with tax questions or a situation where they've clearly outgrown their current tax team. In other words, they started with tax professionals early on in their business who could do the job. Now, their business has grown and expanded many times over, often exponentially, but the tax person has not evolved and grown to the same level as their needs.

Note: this is not always the case, and this is not meant to be a knock on tax professionals. It's just so common that we have to talk about it here: if your original tax person specializes in ultra-small businesses and startups and you've grown into an 8- or 9-figure business, you're going to miss out on a lot of important counsel by keeping with the status quo. I've seen cases where a business expands across many different states and countries, and the tax team is absolutely in over their head. Once the client switched to a new tax team, that former tax person was actually relieved that he was no longer working on their case. It was stressful, and they felt the pressure of advising on issues that were beyond their capabilities. The truly frustrating part is that so many tax professionals simply have their clients submit tax documents once the year is over, then send back the information on how much tax is due and by when. That's almost the extent of their relationship. Maybe there's a couple calls during the year just to check in and see if anything is new, but when you're an entrepreneur, you deserve and need more ongoing communication and strategy around your business and personal taxes throughout the year.

DON'T LEAVE YOUR COUPONS AT HOME

United States Judge Learned Hand once said:

> Anyone may arrange his affairs so that his taxes shall be as low as possible; he is not bound to choose that pattern which best pays the treasury. There is not even a patriotic duty to increase one's taxes. Over and over again the Courts have said that there is nothing sinister in so arranging affairs as to keep taxes as low as possible. Everyone does it, rich and poor alike and all do right, for nobody owes any public duty to pay more than the law demands.

This quote (Helvering v. Gregory, 1934) is often cited in support of the idea that it is not only legal but also acceptable for individuals and corporations to use lawful means to minimize their tax liabilities.

I completely agree with the Judge. Some people feel nervous to say it out loud, but strategic tax planning is a right that you have. The tax code (which is somewhere between 7,000 and 9,000 pages long) is often referred to as a "roadmap" or "playbook" by tax professionals and financial advisors when discussing its role as a guide for taxpayers to legally reduce their taxes. The reason that they call it that is because of the numerous provisions, deductions, credits, and strategies that, when understood and applied correctly, can help individuals and businesses minimize their tax liabilities.

- Roadmap: it's a detailed guide, outlining the routes you can take to navigate the complexities of tax laws, finding legal ways to reduce your tax obligations.
- Playbook: it's also a set of strategies or plans that can be employed to achieve a particular goal—in this case, tax savings.

These metaphors are simple but correct: the code serves as a tool you can legally leverage to keep more of what you earn by paying less in taxes. You can choose to not read it, or you can choose to read it (or have professional experts read it for you) and figure out how to keep more of your money if you do certain things that the government really wants you to do. Take a look at Jeff Bezos. Maybe you've heard of him? Started that little internet-based company called Amazon. As you can imagine, his wealth is largely tied up in Amazon stock (an estimated 85–90 percent, to be exact).

Jeff and other ultra-wealthy entrepreneurs often appear to be in lower tax brackets due to them having their wealth-building largely derived from the appreciation of assets like stocks, rather than traditional income like wages. Does that make him and others unpatriotic or bad citizens? No, it makes them strategic. The tax system in the US primarily taxes realized income, meaning that unless assets are sold and gains are realized, this increase in wealth isn't taxed as income. It's wild to imagine that in some years, Bezos paid zero in federal income taxes despite his wealth increasing by billions of dollars in the same year (because of the rise of his company stock). In other years, he was able to offset his reported income with losses from side investments and other deductions, such as large interest expenses on debts (as we hammered home in the last chapter). In one notable year, his income was offset so much that he even claimed a tax credit for his children, despite a massive increase in net worth! Don't hate the player, hate the game.

Obviously, you and I are not anywhere near Jeff Bezos. But shouldn't we try and learn something from entrepreneurs who are using sophisticated tax planning strategies to keep more of what they earn each year?

Most people don't even pay attention to what's available in the tax code because it's easier to pay the full price and be done with it. So they settle for a tax person to just send them the information right before it's time to pay their bill. Then they complain about how they made all this money but had to pay too much of it in taxes. There's definitely an alternative: find professionals who can explain the ways the government wants to incentivize you as investors and entrepreneurs. If you invest in those incentivized areas, you can pay less in taxes. So why not be proactive, get ahead of the game, and make strategic decisions in your business throughout the year so that the following year you get to keep more of what you worked so hard to earn?

If I were a CPA professional, I'd actually frame it like this to people: "Look, there are 77,000 coupons available, and you can choose how many you want to use—or you can use none of them. It's up to you. But I can teach you how to use the right coupons based on your situation."

Here's a real-life example: The 100 percent bonus depreciation allowed under the Tax Cuts and Jobs Act enabled businesses to fully deduct the cost of eligible assets in the year they were placed in service, up to 2022. After 2022, the deduction phases out, decreasing by 20 percent annually until it ends in 2027. It was essentially a significant federal coupon to buy something for your business with a major tax benefit. Knowing that this rule was going to begin phasing out, dropping from 100 to 80 to 60 percent, I was discussing options with my professional tax team of what my business needed that could take advantage of this opportunity before the "coupon" expired. Before the year was over, I actually bought a private jet and a large office building, both significant assets that could benefit from the bonus depreciation laws.

Chad and his new jet in Florida.

But if you're not aware of these deals and opportunities, you don't get to use the coupons. That's why you need someone who knows how to read the whole coupon book and apply it to your specific situation. There are some coupons that allow you to get something almost for free, but you need to know about them.

If you have a strategic financial team with experience advising high-level entrepreneurs, they can make you aware of all the coupons available, when they expire, and how to best use them for your personal and business financial situation. Without this, you'll miss out on significant opportunities to keep more of what you earn.

> *"Small businesses and entrepreneurs must understand the importance of tax planning. It's not just for the big players; strategic tax management can make a world of difference for startups too."*
>
> **–JACK MA**

W-2 EMPLOYEE ADVISORS VERSUS ENTREPRENEUR ADVISORS

A traditional employee advisor is a W-2 employee who is personally very familiar with the financial circumstances of W-2 employees. Their own tax returns look nothing like yours. They have their taxes withheld from their bi-weekly paycheck, and they pay the difference between what's owed and what was withheld at the end of the year.

If you don't follow the advice of any other chapter in this book, this is the one you better pay attention to. If you're taking financial, tax and strategic wealth advice from a traditional W-2 employee, you could be missing out on potentially millions of dollars of free coupons. These people don't even shop at the same store as you and can't use the same coupons you can use. You've got to remember, you're wired differently.

As an entrepreneur, you need a good understanding of your payroll, all the entities that you own your businesses in, and the tax implications of all your business decisions. If your tax planning is overly simple and the advice is rigid and linear like many traditional financial people are, you won't see so many opportunities right in front of you.

As stated earlier, the US tax code is massive. If you're not getting proactive strategic advice, you're simply paying the maximum retail amount and leaving the coupon book unused. My gut says that doesn't sit well with you, knowing you could be keeping more of your hard-earned money.

The tax and legal complexities that arise as you grow your successful business will cause you to require more support than can be offered by your original bookkeepers and CPAs. Look how far you've come! Congratulations! You've outgrown some people in your life; nothing wrong with that. Now you need to upgrade the professionals around you to be at your level. It's way more common than you might think.

HIRING YOUR FAMILY

Some tax coupons available to you include putting your children and your spouse on your business's payroll and having them do work for your company. (You may already be familiar with this strategy, but it wasn't as common even just a few years ago.)

Even if it's as simple as being part of your marketing department and showing up to company events, being featured in your newsletters, or doing simple work around your office, your kids can be paid by your company. In 2024, dependent children can earn up to $14,600 from employment without needing to file a tax return for

Chad and his family at the Entrepreneur of the Year Awards in Southern CA in 2021.

that income. With earned income, your kids can then contribute to Roth IRAs and 401k retirement plans at a very young age. With compound interest and many decades ahead of them, that money will grow exponentially. For the portion of that income that you don't choose to invest, you could use it for your kids' extracurricular activities or other expenses related to your kids. Why not involve them in some budget planning at their young age? If you're currently paying expenses for your kids anyway, why not have them do some work for your business, earn some money, invest a portion of it, and pay some of their own expenses from their newly acquired tax-free income? As I mentioned earlier, this is exactly what my wife and I have done with our five children.

If you don't have an entrepreneur guiding you financially, you likely wouldn't know all the ins and outs of that type of strategy. As always, consult with your tax and financial professionals before implementing any ideas shared in this book (preferably use one who's also an entrepreneur like you)!

IGNORE THE PANDERING AND RHETORIC

There's no shame in finding legal and allowable strategies to reduce your taxes. When the elite and some politicians make comments about people not "paying their fair share," that's simply a case of pandering to those followers and voters who aren't well-informed about tax laws, finances, and investments. They get people fired up with misinformation and misdirection while they themselves are likely using the very strategies they're condemning in public.

The typical politician pays a lower tax rate than someone working an hourly retail job because much of their personal money is also tied up in investments. So when a wealthy politician says they agree that the wealthy should pay more taxes, they're trying to get other people to pay more, not themselves. They're really saying people who earn a lot through work and paid wages should pay more. Meanwhile, they still have loopholes for themselves to own investments and not pay high taxes.

It's all rhetoric, but it's so pleasing to the ears when someone is sitting on the couch watching TV. A typical voter hears about higher taxes on income and thinks that sounds like a great idea and very fair, not realizing that high earners already pay a very high rate, many reaching a marginal tax rate of 50 percent or higher! At some point, extremely high tax rates start to disincentivize work. And if the federal and state government tax entrepreneurs to the point that they no longer want to work and grow, then all the people they employ will also lose their jobs. Fun fact: as of March 8, 2024, according to Federal Reserve Economic Data, over 134 million Americans are employed by a privately owned business. That's more than half of adults in this country! So it's a very wise thing for the government to give tax incentives and opportunities to the courageous men and women who start and buy businesses to employ those 134 million people.

I believe the real solution to unleash growth and bless everyone is actually to lower tax rates. Lowering tax rates incentivizes growth and innovation. Imagine the impact on the creative entrepreneur class, freeing up more money to expand business, create more jobs, and drive growth around the world.

Wealth Wired Differently

When you buy a jet, for example, think of all the different kinds of workers and specialists who are involved. You've got aerospace engineers who designed the aircraft, assembly line workers built it, and quality control specialists who ensured its safety. Once operational, you've got pilots and pilot trainers, ground crew, airtower control, many teams of mechanics, maintenance and safety groups, etc. Then you've got the sales and customer service representatives managing the transactions and client relationships, all the vendors who support flights and transportation needs, aviation tool companies, airport services, traffic control, etc. This aviation ecosystem illustrates the significant employment and economic contribution beyond the initial purchase of a jet. My pilots have great job security and make a lot more money than if they were working on a contract basis. They're instead part of our business, with full-time salaries, medical benefits, and retirement plans for their families. All of these people (and many more) have work because of the private aviation markets.

> *"Success in business is about mastery, including your tax planning. Master your taxes, and you'll master a key part of your business's financial health."*
>
> **–TONY ROBBINS**

So yes, it's trendy and politically appealing to try to continue to raise the taxes on high earners, but most people don't really consider the widespread economic impact of that entrepreneur. Fewer than 1 percent of the country creates the bulk of the jobs that exist today. Those people—people like me and you—run the American economy. If you're crushed by ever-increasing taxes, everyone's out of luck.

WHY A COMPREHENSIVE PLAN MATTERS

One of our clients sold their business not too long ago. When we dug into his business and tax planning prior to the sale, we found it was a C-corporation, which meant he'd have some specific planning opportunities, including a special rule that would help eliminate capital gains tax on the sale of his business. We connected him with a very qualified tax team that we work with who then prepared his company for the sale. That one planning strategy helped him retain many millions extra in the deal after it closed. Being able to identify the opportunity ahead of time came from our experience with specializing in entrepreneurial clients.

Another client sold his company for over $50 million less than a year ago. He started out as an air-conditioning repair person and grew his business into a highly successful HVAC company. While he was in the process of selling his company to a large national HVAC corporation, he got referred to us to help his family manage their wealth. At the time, he and his wife had zero investment or tax experience.

All of his net worth was tied up in his small business, which is very common. They didn't have a lot of liquid worth and didn't earn a high income, so they'd done no significant wealth or estate planning. We helped their family through the entire sale process and then helped them purchase two commercial real estate properties without using a single dollar of their own money.

By leveraging his investment base and borrowing against it, we worked with his tax team to help accelerate the depreciation of the new buildings. That resulted in them retaining significant amounts of money from the proceeds of his sale that year. We also helped him and his wife set up a real estate business for her to manage the properties. She began helping run that business, and they even hired their two older children to assist her. By including her and their two older sons in the business, we were able to help them retain significant earnings and set up some excellent tax-deferred retirement accounts for the family members.

Just this week, our team was on a conference call with some new clients who are selling a portion of their business with a valuation of close to $900 million. The amount of professional firepower and expertise on that call was so impressive! The experience of being on the inside of these calls for decades is invaluable because each time we work through a deal, we expand our strategies and capabilities to help the entrepreneurial clients we serve or will serve in the future.

We have another client who runs a very successful business that has been in the family for more than seventy years and is now worth $300 million. They would be facing a sizable estate tax due to the growing value of their business and real estate. They want to make sure the next generations of the family can continue to successfully run the business long after they're gone. We implemented some estate and business planning strategies to reduce and then pay for the future estate taxes, allowing them to keep more of their net worth in the family—which, ultimately, allows the business to continue serving communities all across the country.

While employee advisors might focus on standard tax-saving strategies, if any, an entrepreneurial advisor knows how to take a more creative and strategic approach and think through the long-term implications of different kinds and timing of investments. You need someone with real experience to create a comprehensive plan.

KEY TAKEAWAYS

‣ We find most tax professionals have clients turn in their information once the year is over, and then they, in turn, send the tax bill back to the clients after all documents are gathered and calculations are done. That's the extent of the relationship. There's one problem, though: people who don't deal in the entrepreneurial space don't have your same tax situation, so how can they advise you? A traditional employee advisor is a W-2 employee who advises W-2 employees like themselves. Their own tax returns don't look like yours. They can't use the same "coupons" you can use.

‣ There should be no shame or secrecy in finding legal strategies to reduce your taxes. When people in the spotlight make comments about others not "paying their fair share," they're typically pandering to those who aren't well-informed about tax laws or business finance. The tax code is full of coupons you can use. Why work with an advisor who leaves those coupons at home when you go to the store?

‣ While traditional employee financial advisors might focus on standard tax-saving strategies, if any, an entrepreneurial advisor knows how to take a strategic approach and think through the long-term implications of different kinds and timing of investments.

*"An entrepreneur is someone
who jumps off a cliff and
builds a plane on the way down."*

—REID HOFFMAN

CHAPTER 6

Reject the Traditional Career Path Planning

The linear career path to retirement does not apply to people like you and me.

We've already talked about how Jesse Itzler, whom I introduced in Chapter 3, has paved his own way. When he started off as a rapper, he was going place to place, trying to sell his albums. Now he's a multi-millionaire many times over as a co-founder, owner, and partner in many businesses. Then there's Elon Musk, who went from starting Zip2, X.com, and PayPal to SpaceX, Tesla, Solar City, Open AI, and many more. Think of all the massively successful, innovative entrepreneurs with a similar story: Sara Blakely of Spanx, Reid Hoffman of LinkedIn, Richard Branson of Virgin, and the list goes on. They are purpose- and passion-driven, and they've founded and co-founded many successful businesses, completely rejecting a linear career path.

Many entrepreneurs are driven by a sense of purpose or passion for their product, service, or the problem they aim to solve. As an entrepreneur, you sometimes have a hard time explaining exactly what you do for work. In your younger years, your family might have worried about you and harped on you to go get a "real job." But that didn't discourage you or knock you off course: your inner motivation rises above the fear of not having traditional job security that many seek out. The common incentives of job titles and job promotions, bonuses, salaries, and just getting to retirement to lounge around on cruise vacations or golf every day of the week doesn't apply to people like us.

You're here because you feel passion about solving big problems and because you know there's a better way. You want to know who you're impacting, not just what the job title and medical benefits are. You're willing to grind for a long time without any guarantee that it will work out. You may not even be able to get a real pay day for months or years. Choosing to be an entrepreneur, you gave up that safe plan for something much riskier . . . a pursuit to do it your own way and maybe even change a little part of the world along the way.

NO GOLDEN PARACHUTE

When I left Merrill Lynch to start Pacific Capital, I was 32 years old, with a wife, a growing family, a mortgage, and lots of expenses from living in pricey Southern California. Still, I left my very comfortable job because I felt like I wasn't making the impact that I was capable of making.

I had accumulated just over $700,000 of Merrill Lynch company stock as part of my compensation plan, and leaving for any reason would forfeit all of that. It was a very difficult decision, but in my gut, I knew I wasn't destined to stay at the Big Wall Street Bank my whole life. I didn't fit in there. I remember resigning on a Monday morning, and on Tuesday, when I logged into my stock account, the balance showed $0. It felt like such a gut punch, even though I figured that's what would happen. As is their M.O., they always file a lawsuit against their elite wealth managers who leave, trying to create as many roadblocks and obstacles to future success. They also don't want the financial advisor's clients to ever leave the big bank and follow their advisor. That means on top of being a new entrepreneur responsible for a lease, office equipment, payroll, etc., I had significant legal bills to pay.

This was a challenging time for me and my family, and most non-entrepreneur peers would be wondering why I'd even put myself in this situation in the first place. I felt overwhelmed, frustrated, and stressed from both a personal and financial standpoint. *I did everything right, followed all company and industry procedures to resign and start my own business. I followed the protocol 100% and communicated properly with my management,* I thought. *My attorney even said I was so overly compliant that I made it harder on myself than it needed to be. What a mess.*

I gave up my 7-figure annual income, all the corporate perks, and wiped away my entire stock account at the age of 32, because my passion and a dream of making a bigger impact with the freedom to serve clients how they wanted to be served mattered more to me.

Being an employee of the big bank was so restrictive that I felt unable to be my true self and make an impact on the clients I served. I waved goodbye to those traditional career motivators and all that security and name brand recognition, even though some family and close friends thought it was too risky. I instead jumped to a place of complete insecurity and uncertainty, but it was where I was most passionate and could create the biggest impact.

I wanted the freedom to be absolutely transparent with entrepreneurial clients, which I couldn't be before. I'm not a rigid suit-and-tie-wearing corporate PowerPoint presenter. If I continued playing a part that wasn't authentic, I'd never live up to my full potential. So I had to make the leap, at the expense and sacrifice of a great deal of money, security, and predictability. Once on my own, I could just be myself.

Maybe you can relate. Maybe you've had a moment, too, when you needed to step out of a comfortable life and say, "Here I go." That's why we understand each other so well. We've both been there, looking over the edge of the high dive way down at the pool below and asking ourselves, "Am I really gonna jump?"

"After playing five years in the NFL, I pivoted into a career in business where I have been able to leverage my experience in working on high-performing NFL teams to provide a unique perspective on how to manage organizations.

When I transitioned into business, I joined a management consulting firm (BCG) where I felt out of place since my peers had spent years working in Excel, Powerpoint, and cranking out emails. I came to the table with knowledge of blocking schemes that were useless to our clients. It felt like I would never catch up with those that followed a traditional path into business. I thought the best path was to try to be more like those on that well-worn ladder, but I really accelerated in my career when I realized that imitating traditionalists was limiting me. As soon as I recognized what skills I learned in the NFL were applicable to business, I was able to quickly generate positive impact by leading teams to better compete in the market. Now I am leading a PE-backed industrial flow control distribution company with over 1,000 team members in 50 locations.

While I am not a founder, I have worked with a PE sponsor to create a holding company that is a platform of businesses which is a form of entrepreneurship. For me, it is important to partner with people who have a similar mindset and are looking to grow and align goals with me."

—SCOTT JACKSON, CEO OF FLOWORKS

YOU'RE NOT ON THE LINEAR PATH

The traditional financial advice would be to follow the well-paved path along your career, get promoted, and eventually find complete security via the benefits of tenure at your company or in your industry. This is the more common, linear path toward a successful career and eventual retirement. But that's not the path you're on. That kind of life probably sounds boring to you anyway, so the advice for that path doesn't apply to you at all.

One of our clients went to a prestigious medical school and became a well-respected surgeon. However, less than a decade into that career, he decided it wasn't for him. He just didn't love it and couldn't see himself in a white coat doing medical procedures for the rest of his life. He completely pivoted, went back to business school, began work at a prestigious business consulting firm, and eventually started his own project management and consulting company. His new company would focus on specifically Fortune 500 biotech and pharmaceutical companies. He's since grown his business to over 1,200 employees and an enterprise value of over $150 million. Nothing he did followed a logical or linear path. A traditional employee advisor may have counseled him not to throw away the $300,000 of medical school expenses and the many years spent to become a surgeon just to switch to a business career! But he's so much happier now, doing exciting things in the business world and traveling to meet clients and their teams all over the world.

Another client's family business was started in the 1970s in Southern California. The founder went to law school as a newlywed, but then when it was time to take the bar exam, he realized he didn't want to be a lawyer. It was very disappointing to his parents and spouse after all the sacrifice and expense of preparing for the exam and going to school for years. While he was looking for his next opportunity, he started picking up recyclable trash in the back of his pickup truck just to pay some small bills until he figured out what he really wanted to be when he grew up. That odd side job turned into a giant recycling company—a family business that employed many family members and still exists to this day, 50 years later. Traditional thinking would've said, "Don't throw away your law degree or all the time you've spent preparing! How could you possibly not take the bar exam and follow through with this? You'd be so successful as a lawyer."

A real entrepreneur, though, doesn't settle or succumb to the sunk-cost fallacy. If you have that abundant, exponential mindset, you know you might need to try 10 or 100 ideas before you hit the bullseye and find what you're truly passionate about. It's okay to think differently from the traditional naysayers, to try, fail, and try again—in fact, it's a gift.

You can teach your kids the same thing. It's okay to try and fail. In fact, it's necessary for your growth and development. Don't teach your kids to be know-it-alls; teach them instead to be learn-it-alls. If you have a perfectionist mentality, you won't learn from your failures . . . you may actually avoid even attempting things, which I'd say is more of a failure than trying something new and it not working. That's why social media often gets a bad rap; it's just a highlight reel of perfectly filtered successes and wins when life isn't supposed to be so neat and tidy. The traditional concept of graduating high school,

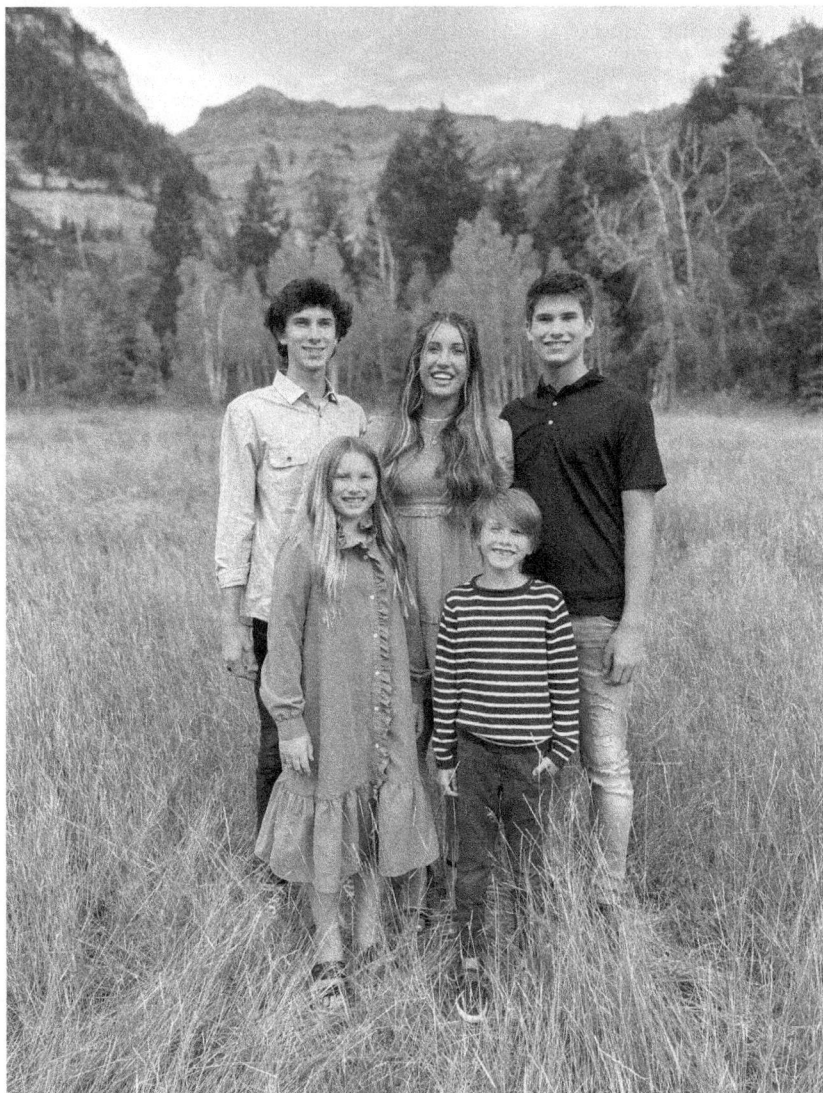

The Willardson kids in Sundance, Utah, 2023.

getting good grades, going to university, choosing a good major, getting a good job, blah, blah, blah . . . that's linear perfectionism, all up and no down.

Real life doesn't work that way (thank goodness it doesn't). You'll have false starts and steps back. You'll fall down. Remember when you were a baby, learning to walk? Ok, do you at least remember witnessing your own child or some young child in your life learning to walk? What did they do after they fell down and sat their diaper back on the floor? Did they just decide it was the wrong path to do this new "walking" thing that others are doing? Or did they resolve that they'd keep trying until they figured it out? Life is supposed to be full of experiences just like that little baby or toddler learning to walk. You're supposed to fall down. And eventually, when you're learning to ride a bike, you're going to have times where you fall off and scrape your knee. My wife and I believe that's good for our kids—they need to fall down and scrape their knees and learn that they'll survive and be okay.

And in case you're reading this and thinking to yourself, "This is more applicable to younger entrepreneurs and risk-takers. I'm at an age now where I'm not trying many new things or stepping outside my comfort zone as much anymore," just know that it's all in your head. There are plenty of famous entrepreneurs who started after age fifty or who didn't hit their bullseye until later in life: Henry Ford was 45 when he created the Model T. A recent success, Jamie Kern Lima, founder of IT Cosmetics, is in her forties and has been named to Forbes's list of "America's Richest Self-Made Women" since 2017. It's never too late to go big.

"My business career has been mission-based. Maximally based, all in, for service. I am looking forward to working with a wealth advisory team that understands mission-based entrepreneurship. What perhaps makes my entrepreneurial story unique started with becoming a missionary. I had been in practice for 5 years as a dentist when I left and sold everything I had built up until that time and left it behind . . . for 1/6th the salary. High-risk living in West Africa. The first step is always giving! The 5 years there in Africa as a dental missionary, dedicated to serving, changed my mindset! It truly paved the way to abundance in health and wealth in later years, and for that I am so thankful.

Being on a mission gives you unnatural, laser focus!"

–CHRIS NEIBAUER, DDS,

  FOUNDER AND CEO OF ABUNDANT DENTAL CARE

CHOOSE TO STAY IN THE GAME

If your "financial advisor" is also an entrepreneur, they'll understand your primary goal is not to stay on the safe, incremental straight-and-narrow. They'll also understand you may never retire. You'll always be coming up with new ideas or jumping into new opportunities, whether you're 55 or 75 years old. Instead of trying to fit you into their planning calculator equations, they'll be more open and flexible toward new ideas and your unconventional path. A stagnant retirement of sitting around on the couch and watching the news is not in your DNA. You're always going to be engaged and doing new things. You're wired differently.

We have a very new client who found us after reading my most recent book *Fit for Wealth*. He's 73 years old and has an energy and enthusiasm for life that's completely on fire. He's always joking around and keeping conversations lively. He's excited about growth.

Chad being interviewed on ABC News in 2023 for his new book, Fit for Wealth.

He's got huge goals for the new year, and he's trying to grow his business, Abundant Dental Care, to 9 figures. He splits his time between South Florida and Park City, Utah. He's not retiring; he's not sitting around sipping his coffee and reading the newspaper, reminiscing on the "good ole days." His calendar is full of activity; he's growing, hiring, mentoring, consulting, and acquiring other dental practices. He says many of his peers are in wheelchairs and rocking chairs because they decided they should retire and they "stopped going for stuff." By staying active, he's making an impact and adding to his legacy.

Wouldn't you want your kids and grandkids to see you thriving at age 73? Instead of fading into the sunset, show them what's possible and what they can aspire to. One major advantage of working with an entrepreneurial advisor is that they are likely aiming for the same things as you and understand the power of legacy-building and continuous value-creation. You can't put a price on that sort of understanding.

KEY TAKEAWAYS

▸ The traditional incentives of job promotions, bonuses, steady salaries, and just getting to retirement to have more time for golf or reading the newspaper do not apply to entrepreneurs. We're wired differently. Your advisor should understand that your path has never been, and will never be, that linear.

▸ If you have an abundant, exponential mindset, you know you might need to try 10 or 100 ideas before you hit the bullseye and find what you're truly passionate about. It's okay to think differently from the traditional naysayers, to try, fail, and try again—in fact, it's a gift.

▸ Have you had a moment when you needed to step out of a comfortable life and say, "Here I go?" An entrepreneurial advisor has had that moment—maybe even more than one of those moments, in fact—and they can help light your path forward. Be intentional about who you ask for help when it comes to big questions like your future and your legacy, and don't take advice from someone you wouldn't trade places with.

"You are the average of the five people you spend the most time with. Choose wisely to foster an environment of mutual growth and idea exchange."

—JIM ROHN

CHAPTER 7

Exchange Ideas with a True Entrepreneurial Thought Partner

Being an entrepreneur is often a lonely gig. You don't have a lot of people you can talk to about what's going on inside your head. You may be going through a variety of things: feeling burned out and overworked, being excited about your brand new idea, or just looking to celebrate a huge win in your business.

Who is your "thought partner" for your entrepreneurial ideas, struggles, wins, and crucial financial decision-making moments for your business? I've heard some clients even share that this thought partnership and idea exchange might be one of the most valuable services we provide to entrepreneurs, even above the wealth management work we do. For example, we have a client in Switzerland who built a large global business with his brother. The company has grown to have employees all over the world in many different time zones. He works a hundred hours a week and seemingly has no room for a personal or social life because he's always had it in his mind that he needs to have a certain amount of money in the bank before he is "successful." I challenged him on what he actually wants versus what he's pursuing, and I pointed out he's basically killing himself and unable to pursue anything outside of just putting his head down and working on his business.

Through that conversation where I challenged him on what kind of net worth he really wants and the cost required to get there, he's shifted his mindset regarding what he actually needs in order to be comfortable and financially free. We've worked on creative ways to hire, delegate, and bring on more executive leaders in both the US and Europe so that he can get his health and personal freedom back. He's now much happier and healthier because of that shift.

The depth of that conversation is not one a traditional employee advisor is going to be able to reach with an entrepreneur like you. Why? Because he or she has not gone through that same battle themselves.

> *When it comes to our clients, we're not just financial advisors or business partners— we are essential thought partners. There's no language barrier between us. We are fluent in entrepreneurship.*

My team is familiar with how you think and operate because they deal with me all the time. They work in an entrepreneurial environment every day. Instead of serving as nothing more than number crunchers and professional investors, we help our clients live more fulfilling lives outside just operating their businesses. We help them pause, reflect on, and celebrate their wins. The exponential mindset involves continuing to grow and evolve as a high-level entrepreneur, which requires having peers who understand you, who can challenge you, and with whom you can openly express your ridiculous ambition.

Just because you have lots of money or a very high income doesn't prevent you from getting lonely. In fact, you might be more lonely because almost no one can relate to you. You're still human with all the emotions that entails. I remember sending a text to a client, basically telling him why I admire him and his wife and what a great family they are. I told him what others have mentioned to me about them recently and the impact they have on the community. He called me almost immediately after receiving my text, so quickly that it startled me. He confessed that he was struggling and having a really tough week, and that my text couldn't have come at a more perfect time. Nobody would've ever guessed that this leader was struggling. He and his wife are always in the spotlight and expected to be the rock that others lean on.

On the flip side, highly successful business owners often don't have anyone to celebrate wins with. Their wins are so big and unrelatable that they feel embarrassed even sharing them with anyone. Some clients call me to celebrate, saying, "You're the only person I feel like I can tell this to, but man, I landed this huge deal today and I've been giving all my blood, sweat, and tears toward this opportunity. It finally happened!" Don't underestimate the value of having that one person or that team you can confide in and speak openly with about anything you're experiencing as an entrepreneur or entrepreneurial couple. That relationship and connection are very valuable.

It's stifling to have an entrepreneur's brain but constantly run up against the limited thinking, pessimism, or scarcity mentality of the typical world. If you don't find supporters, circles, and outlets for your gifted uniqueness, it will feel like living in a prison. Working with an entrepreneurial advisor can set you free.

WE'LL CHALLENGE YOU TO ACHIEVE

If you're talking to a financial professional who is not even remotely on your level, they'll never challenge you to achieve more, and they won't be able to relate to what you're going through or how you think.

In fact, they may be uncomfortable with how big you think. They might say you've done enough and don't need to go for more because your giant vision even makes them uncomfortable. There's a limit to the abundance thinking of many people you're talking to. Taking advice from them will influence what you're willing to go for and what you think is possible. Recently, I was in a meeting with a new client. He's very sharp and has had 3 to 4 business exits, with this most recent one valued at close to $200 million. One aspect he appreciates in our conversations is that I've challenged him on some of his assumptions and goals, including things he was anchored to that were going to impact what their family can spend and do right now. When I challenged him and really pushed back, he replied with, "Wow, those were some really great thoughts. You're giving me permission to let go of some beliefs that would really hold us back."

That's the whole point. As an ambitious and creative entrepreneur, you're used to being the misfit in the group. But what if you weren't the misfit at all? What if your big new ideas were fully supported by a team of smart business financial experts who totally get you? Hopefully, you have those kinds of networks or you run in those kinds of circles where your creativity and big ideas can be fully expressed with other people just like you. I started my ELEVATED (Platinum Elevated™) entrepreneur coaching program to gather and mentor exactly this type of group of go-getters. When you're in a room full of people with unreasonable goals, your unreasonable goals suddenly feel very reasonable. If you surround yourself with people who also have an abundant possibility mentality, then you're more apt to try big things.

Remember, thought partnership comes from travel guides who have been on the adventure you want to take and understand why the challenge excites you. They don't try to talk you out of it or steer you toward something smaller, simpler, and safer. Travel agents may not even like their job, let alone have any personal experience of undertaking the journey and excursions you're headed toward. You'll have way more fun going on the excursion with someone who loves that path and knows a ton about it because that's all they've been doing their whole life. Having someone to champion and support your ideas can help you clarify how to get there and challenge you to reach for more.

If you surround yourself with people who just say yes or don't ever challenge you and engage like a peer, you won't grow much. Most financial people who are not entrepreneurs and not at your level probably won't push back on your ideas. They won't know how to help you navigate the minefield. I'm very comfortable pushing back and telling ultra-wealthy clients that their idea is bad, misguided, biased, dangerous, or that they don't understand what they're talking about. Smart, wealthy people actually appreciate that candor. They know even if they don't like what I have to say, they can rely on me giving them the straight truth (with nothing but good intentions).

WE'RE ON THE SAME WAVELENGTH

One philosophy I've taught a lot in coaching entrepreneurs and entrepreneurial couples is that in your marriage and your business partnerships, you don't always need to agree, but you do need to be aligned. You'll recall that we discussed this earlier in Chapter 3.

When you're on the same wavelength with your entrepreneurial advisor, you can really come up with great ideas and strategies together. You're not limited in what you can talk about or afraid of diving deep into what business challenges you're trying to work through. You can bring up a hiring scenario, questions about expansion, or concerns about letting people go, and you'll receive useful input (and maybe some fresh ideas). Your entrepreneurial advisor won't

"An entrepreneurial advisor team like Pacific Capital provides me with pushback on my ideas and thoughts. They can do research or sit in investment presentations that help me make decisions. It allows me to replicate the successful pattern my business had in mergers and acquisitions around my private investments.

It's important to have a thought partner with experience in what I'm going through. Although I strive to be able to learn from anyone (a true learner doesn't need a superior or a great teacher to learn), it sometimes is hard. When discussing investments with those who are ignorant of my success and condescending to me or with those who have not achieved personal success, I find myself struggling to extract their points from my emotions regarding their experience. This makes it unnecessarily hard to hear them and learn from them. When my opposite number is also a successful peer, that obstacle is removed and the friction is removed from learning. Bottom line, it is easier to learn from someone you admire."

—CASEY ADAMS, CO-FOUNDER OF
VISIBLE SUPPLY CHAIN MANAGEMENT

give you a blank look and quickly go back to talking about the markets. They'll actually get excited to consult on the entrepreneurial questions you're bringing to the table. That's because they're wired differently, just like you. It's a great feeling knowing you can speak freely about what you're dealing with, about things too confidential to take to your team members and employees.

Traditional employee advisors are uncomfortable with thinking "too big" or "outside the box" when you bring them a ridiculous new idea that will cost a lot of money and time. I've seen them dismiss entrepreneurs as not being able to focus. To an outsider, you seem like you're all over the place and can't sit still or be tamed. You don't fit in the "sit down and shut up" culture (that's been engrained through years of traditional schooling). That approach won't work for you.

When there's no language barrier, you have more opportunities that come from real connection, as my clients found when we brought them new investors for their car wash venture. An entrepreneurial advisor has a deep entrepreneurial network and the ability to make introductions for you and your business. It's been said that your net worth is your network. The introductions I've been able to make among people have yielded amazing results for them. I've got no financial incentive to do so, but it's what entrepreneurs do for each other! We make valuable connections and hook people up with business and investment opportunities. When your mindset is in the abundant possibility state all the time, all you see are opportunities. You connect people who need to meet, and cool things happen.

Maybe you've heard that entrepreneurs are often C students who struggle in the classroom because they're put in a box in the school system and told to sit down and be quiet—all when they're constantly thinking of new ideas or different ways to do things. Maybe their mind is wandering or questioning what's happening and why. The traditional education system teaches kids not to speak unless spoken to, not to collaborate, to study and take tests all by themselves, and to focus on individual achievement above all else. In the real world, though, collaboration wins. When you learn to build teams and solve big issues together, you can create lots of magic. And when you need help, it's not cheating to ask for it. Collaborating, connecting, and networking are the greatest keys to success.

Yes, business can be competitive, but it really runs on relationships and mutual support. If you know there's plenty to go around, you don't need to hide opportunities from people or keep connections to yourself. You can share them freely.

So many of my followers and connections on LinkedIn are also financial advisors. At first, I felt a little guarded—why were they always commenting on my stuff and asking me questions? Are they trying to see what I do and say to clients? Are they looking to take my ideas and copy them? Then, after a little bit of reflection, I realized the answer doesn't really matter. It was a complete mindset shift when I really sat with that idea. This was back around 2013 or 2014 when I was initially really engaging on LinkedIn. I came to the conclusion that there are more than enough clients in the world for every financial professional to be successful. That is the definition of abundant thinking. The more open I am, the larger my audience becomes, and the more the opportunities appear to connect with or help others around me. Unlike many of my "competitors," I'm not worried about scrapping and competing anymore, so we can just have healthy conversations and help each other with the challenges and struggles we face. We approach our clients with that same abundance mentality.

"Chad and his team are more than advisors; our values align and they see my success as their own. Unlike others who only look one way, they see the full picture of my business and life, ensuring decisions benefit all aspects. Plus, they're just a text away, making complex advice straightforward and immediate.

The best advice I've ever received is to only take advice from those with actual results. That's why I chose Chad; he's an entrepreneur, not your typical wealth advisor. His entrepreneurial success across numerous ventures allows me to trust him and his team in their financial guidance."

–MICHAEL MOGILL, FOUNDER AND CEO, CRISP

WE CAN TALK ABOUT REAL BUSINESS QUESTIONS

An entrepreneurial advisor can offer advice on all aspects of your business, well beyond your investment and banking accounts or loans. This includes things like expanding locations or services, building a culture, adding a product line, training executives, dealing with HR challenges, collaborating with other wealth-builders outside your business, navigating hiring are all core to your success outside of discussions about the markets, and more. For instance, clients often ask me, "How'd you find such great executive assistants?" I used to work at a big bank and felt so entrapped by the rigid structures there, but now I can form my own team—a responsibility I take very seriously. To hire the two superstar assistants I have now, I followed a very thorough screening process, gave them more than a couple specific assessments, and structured their training in an intentional way.

My hiring process has worked so well that in February 2024, my two assistants and I flew to Florida to speak on stage at a large conference for elite entrepreneurs. People wanted to hear about why two executive assistants are better than one, how I've made that arrangement work, and how we have a triangle of responsibility and accountability. They both do very different things for me—there's no overlap—but we're all aligned in our goals. I describe one assistant as my "right brain" and one as my "left brain. My "left brain" assistant Maddie naturally handles all the left-brain work: business relationships, business vendors, financial stuff, taxes, real estate management, and new business projects. My "right brain" assistant Oriya is all right brain: handling media, PR, newsletters, personal hospitality, family support, and travel.

Chad, Dan Sullivan, and his two primary executive assistants, Oriya and Maddie speaking on stage at Entrepreneur Conference in Florida, 2024.

They're both very professional, responsive, supportive, ambitious, and aligned, but they fill very different roles. For example, when I write and publish a new book, Oriya's involved in the marketing campaign, setting up interviews and book signings, book cover image design, content ideas, distribution, and helping encourage readers to review my book on Amazon. Maddie, on the other hand, works on the publishing contracts, the audiobook recording, the back-end logistics with Amazon and bookstore vendors, and business issues like that. As an entrepreneur, I've found there's a major advantage and benefit to being highly conscious of what people's strengths and weaknesses are and how you can work together to optimize their talents and gifts. No one working for me feels like they're *working* or *grinding through* things they don't enjoy. Everyone loves what they do. They're happy and engaged. They only work on their favorite things—things that they're very good at and energized by—instead of struggling and enduring some tasks they hate and aren't skilled at. The benefit for the entrepreneur when you set your team up for success like this is that you don't have to be over-managing or worried if their work is getting done. They love doing what they're doing, so they initiate more solutions and create more success than if you would've been over their shoulder micromanaging each step of the way.

You can have that exact same setup, too. An entrepreneurial advisor can guide you in your unique situation to diagnose what you and your business need most. They'll offer wisdom around delegating and collaborating in such a way that you can maximize both your business and your personal enjoyment of life. A traditional employee advisor could not do that; they're not assembling organizations and building teams, hiring and training new people, managing payroll, etc. That's just not the world they're living in. If you're trying to elevate your business to the next level through better hiring, training, and retention, or you're rolling out a brand new product or service, there is nothing more annoying than someone yammering in your ear about the stock market and what their prediction is about how it will move or what's next for interest rates in the upcoming quarter. (P.S. Even the foolishness of making confident stock market or real estate predictions goes against any good entrepreneur's experience.) You know you can't predict what's going to happen to *your* business over the next few months. How is someone going to do that accurately for the whole global economy?

Yet that's what the typical advisor spends most of their time doing: looking at charts and graphs, predicting what's going to happen, and talking about the markets. You and I both know they're wasting their time guessing and predicting, and we don't want to listen to overly confident people predicting things that can't actually be predicted. It's one of those things about this industry that's always felt foolish to me.

But don't just take my word for it. Check out what some of the most successful investors in history say about it:

- "You never can predict the economy. You can't predict the stock market. "—Peter Lynch
- "We have long felt that the only value of stock forecasters is to make fortune-tellers look good. Even now, Charlie (Munger) and I continue to believe that short-term market forecasts are poison and should be kept locked up in a safe place, away from children and also from grown-ups who behave in the market like children."—Warren Buffett
- "If I have noticed anything over these sixty years on Wall Street, it is that people do not succeed in forecasting what's going to happen to the stock market."—Benjamin Graham
- "Economists' forecasting skill is about as good as guessing. Even the economists that directly or indirectly run the economy (the Federal Reserve, the Council of Economic Advisors, and the Congressional Budget Office) had forecasting records that were worse than pure chance."—William Sherden

When I hear people talk about what's going to happen in the markets, how an election year will change the charts, exactly when the next recession will start, what interest rates will be at the end of the year, and how real estate will behave, I think to myself, *You don't know any of this*. It's like a weatherman who has no clue.

An entrepreneurial advisor would likely be much more open to the uncertainty and unpredictability of what's around the corner because they're aware that all these unknowns exist. They'd likely focus on controlling what you can control, which is designing your business and life to maximize your impact on the world.

The questions about how to get there are the ones worth answering.

KEY TAKEAWAYS

‣ It's stifling to have an entrepreneur's brain but constantly run up against the limited thinking, pessimism, or scarcity mentality of the typical world. If you don't find supporters, circles, and outlets for your gifted uniqueness, it will feel like living in a prison. Working with an entrepreneurial advisor can set you free.

‣ An entrepreneurial advisor can offer advice on all aspects of your business, well beyond cash flow. Things like expanding locations or services, building a culture, adding a product line, and navigating hiring are all core to your success outside of discussions about balance sheets.

‣ An entrepreneurial advisor speaks your language from experience. This takes the pressure off of the client–advisor relationship. You don't have to go to great lengths to explain everything happening under the hood. We can accomplish so much more growth—and make such a bigger impact—when there's no language barrier.

CONCLUSION

"How did you start this business?"

That's what I asked the old farmer standing in front of me. I was 14 or 15 years old, already very curious about businesses—how they started, how they worked. We were standing in his office looking out the window toward his ranch that had millions of chickens at the headquarters of his family farm operation. He'd hired my dad many years ago in his company and promoted him all the way up to the CEO position.

The older gentleman, now in his eighties, told me his personal story as an immigrant and a Holocaust survivor. When he came to the US, he'd started with one chicken. One! And he'd grown the company from there—from one chicken to a large-scale business selling eggs to large grocers and companies all over the country. After he finished telling me a little bit of his story, he pulled me in by the collar and said something I will never forget:

"America is the greatest country in the world because you can start anything here! There's no limits to what you can achieve! Just look at my life. I had nothing. I spoke no English, and now I have a business that's grown all over the US. I have over $100 million dollars, and I came here with NOTHING!"

Needless to say, despite his very short stature, his power and enthusiasm were electric! And he was living proof of his statement. That man was right then, and what he said is still right today. We can start whatever we want here in this land of opportunity. We can build businesses and not only impact the world, but also provide for our families for decades to come. It's exciting to be a creator, to see your big ideas through and recognize how many great opportunities lie at our fingertips, isn't it?

I know you "get" that. An entrepreneurial advisor will "get" that, too. It goes beyond understanding what those words mean on the surface—it's about knowing how it feels to play in this space of high risk and high reward, of possibilities and opportunities. That's what makes this life journey so exciting.

That's why, if you're not working with an entrepreneur who understands this and sees the world like you do, you're missing out on leveraging all the advantages I've covered here in this book. When you upgrade your team to people who are aligned with the work you do and the way you think, you'll have so much more success and so many more opportunities.

I challenge you to get wealth and financial advice from professionals who speak your entrepreneur language fluently. Find someone who's been there before, a travel guide who's personally gone down this path on this exact journey many times before and who's led others on the journey too. You don't want to be the first person they've taken on this excursion. You want someone with the personal experience *and* the leadership experience to give you relevant, valuable advice. That kind of guide will know where the pitfalls and opportunities are. They'll help you create new possibilities with your money and business decisions as an entrepreneur.

We understand the emotional and familial concerns that come up on a challenging journey, and we can provide reassurance because we've already prevailed many times before. We also understand that you want a peer and a partner who knows the ins and outs of the entrepreneurial lifestyle, from the tax implications to the need to celebrate the biggest wins.

Of course, just because you have a guide doesn't mean you won't encounter rough terrain. Having a guide doesn't mean it's going to be perfect weather. But it does mean they have the experience to help you navigate storms and other challenging conditions.

President Franklin Roosevelt said, "A smooth sea never made a skilled sailor." Navigating the waters of entrepreneurship and prevailing with exponential thinking requires the ability to work in the face of uncertainty and uneven cash flow, economic ups and downs, and family emotions and relationships. It requires persevering despite the naysayers and riding out and all the other elements of the entrepreneurial roller coaster. It sounds scary to some, but you and I (and other entrepreneurial advisors out there) see the long-term potential of what we're building—and we wouldn't have it any other way.

ABOUT THE AUTHOR

Chad Willardson, CFF, CRPC®, AWMA®, is the founder and president of Pacific Capital, a fiduciary wealth advisory firm he founded in 2011 after nine years of climbing the ranks as an investment advisor at Merrill Lynch. Chad is also the founder of the entrepreneur coaching program ELEVATED (Platinum Elevated™). His bestselling first book, *Stress-Free Money*, was featured in Forbes's "21 Books To Read In 2021." His second book, *Smart, Not Spoiled* is increasing financial literacy among young people across the country and led to him co-founding the app GravyStack and co-hosting the *Smart Money Parenting* show, which reached the number 2 ranking of all of Apple podcasts in the parenting and family. His third book, *Beyond the Money*, is tailored to the eight- and nine-figure entrepreneurial clients Pacific Capital serves. His fourth book, *Fit for Wealth*, was released in 2023 and is helping entrepreneurs and go-getters find both physical and financial wellness.

Chad is a writer for *Entrepreneur* magazine and serves on the Forbes Business Council for entrepreneurs. In addition to serving the family office clients of Pacific Capital, Chad also manages the $600 million investment portfolio as the elected City Treasurer for the 170,000 residents in his community. Chad is recognized as one of the top wealth management experts in the country and has appeared in the *Wall Street Journal*, Forbes, Inc., NBC News, Yahoo Finance, Nasdaq,

U.S. News & World Report, InvestmentNews, *Entrepreneur*, and *Financial Advisor* magazine and two bestselling books, *Who Not How* and *The Gap and the Gain* by Dan Sullivan, Dr. Benjamin Hardy, and Tucker Max. He's also currently an author for *Entrepreneur*. He earned his bachelor's degree in economics from Brigham Young University in Provo, Utah.

Chad created and trademarked The Financial Life Inspection*, a unique process to remove the stress people feel about their money. Chad is passionate about financial education and believes that with the right tools and resources, people can be empowered to make smart money decisions. As a Certified Financial Fiduciary*, he loves to help people organize their financial life, clarify their goals, and make decisions that lead them to a successful and fulfilling life. As a father of five, teaching children to be smart and not spoiled is especially important to him.

Outside of his business, Chad loves to travel with his family and enjoys playing and watching sports. Chad and his family are very engaged in serving their community. Besides serving as an elected official, he and his family seek out ways to give back to various charitable causes. Chad served as a volunteer for two years on a church service mission in Lithuania, Latvia, Estonia, and Belarus and can speak, read, and write fluently in Lithuanian. Above all, Chad cherishes his family. A native of Orange County, California, Chad and his wife of 22 years live in Southern California with their five beautiful children.

The Willardson family in Sundance, Utah, 2023.